Project Management Institute

D1396616

A Strategic-Oriented Implementation of Projects

Mihály Görög, PhD, Professor of Project Management

Library of Congress Cataloging-in-Publication Data

Görög, Mihály, 1951-
  A strategic-oriented implementation of projects / Mihály Görög, PhD, Professor
of Project Management.
      pages cm
  Includes bibliographical references and index.
  ISBN-13: 978-1-935589-87-7 (alk. paper)
  ISBN-10: 1-935589-87-3 (alk. paper) 1. Project management. 2. Strategic planning.
I. Title.
  HD69.P75G677 2013
  658.4'012—dc23

                          2013015075

ISBN: 978-1-935589-87-7

Published by: Project Management Institute, Inc.
                   14 Campus Boulevard
                   Newtown Square, Pennsylvania 19073-3299 USA
                   Phone: +610-356-4600
                   Fax: +1610-356-4647
                   Email: customercare@pmi.org
                   Internet: www.PMI.org

PMI Publications welcomes corrections and comments on its books. Please feel free to send
comments on typographical, formatting, or other errors. Simply make a copy of the relevant page
of the book, mark the error, and send it to: Book Editor, PMI Publications, 14 Campus Boulevard,
Newtown Square, PA 19073-3299 USA.

To inquire about discounts for resale or educational purposes, please contact the PMI Book
Service Center.
      PMI Book Service Center
      P.O. Box 932683, Atlanta, GA 31193-2683 USA
      Phone: 1-866-276-4764 (within the U.S. or Canada) or +1-770-280-4129 (globally)
      Fax: +1-770-280-4113
      Email: info@bookorders.pmi.org

The paper used in this book complies with the Permanent Paper Standard issued by the National
Information Standards Organization (Z39.48—1984).

10 9 8 7 6 5 4 3 2 1

Table of Contents

List of Figures

List of Tables

Preface

A project can seem successful, but if it doesn't achieve its strategic objective, it ultimately fails.

Working with both national and international clients in the twelve years following graduation, I saw two ultimate reasons for project failure. One of them was the poor definition of the expected project result (especially in case of internal projects), and the other one was the inappropriate use of contracting out projects. These two, apparently different issues are interrelated. Since contracting out a work implies the allocation of risks and responsibilities between the parties, inappropriate definition of the expected project result does not make possible to contract out projects reliably. Appropriate definition of the project result is needed to define the allocation of risks and responsibilities reliably, thus this definition provides a basis for contracting out projects. Consequently, inappropriate definition of the project result also leads to project failure in this way too.

Many times I experienced that the desired project result was not aligned with the beneficial change implied in the underlying strategic objective to be achieved. These situations always have resulted in serious problems, such as lack of client (sponsor) satisfaction, hostile stakeholders, and finally serious time and cost overrun—or even project cancellation. The ultimate reason for these problems was the lack of appropriate approaches and methods which could facilitate practitioners both to define the project outcome and implement the project in a strategy-oriented manner. I also experienced many times in case of external projects that the use of an inappropriate type of contract and type of payment resulted in project disaster, since the project client was unable to control the project implementation process under the conditions. The situation was even more difficult when the misuse of these tools was coupled with the misuse of tendering and prequalification. The ultimate reason for these problems was the prevailing legal approach to contracting out projects, while this issue needed a managerial approach.

Later I started an academic career, and when I got my PhD, I was involved in different projects as a consultant, and I was also active in conducting in-company training courses. During this time, I also experienced that the desired project result was not in compliance with the strategic objective to be achieved. It was especially true in the case of organizational development projects and of IT/IS (information technology/information system) projects. At the same time, I also experienced that the way in which projects were contracted out was often based on organizational usage rather than the actual context of the project.

These two problem areas (i.e., the ultimate reasons I have experienced for project failure) are rooted back to the lack of a strategic-oriented, and, at the same time, practical approach to implementing projects, especially external projects. Extant literature does not address these problems sufficiently. Therefore, my research efforts gradually focused on strategy-oriented scope management of the achievable project result (including the associated success criteria), and the phenomenon of project implementation strategy (contracting out projects) in the broader sense.

This book is based to a great extent on these previous research outcomes, while experiences gained from consultancy and in-company training courses are also utilized in the book.

I hope that those who read this book will find the knowledge gained from it both useful and applicable. This book, however, may contribute to improving professionalism not only in project client organizations (organizations that initiate projects) but in project-based organizations (external contributors) as well, at least in two ways. One of them is when they need to accomplish ill-defined project results for a project client. The other one is when they need to manage their contractor-subcontractor relationships.

Finally, I would like to make an important note that has been refined through experience. The attitude of the project client organization toward the appropriate (i.e., strategy-oriented) scope management is crucial. Time devoted to this issue, especially to a strategy-oriented scope definition of the desired project result, is time well spent. Time and money saved in the early phase of a project will not result in earlier completion. On the contrary, it can lead to both time and cost overruns, and to a project result that may not contribute to achieving the desired strategic objective which the project is based on. Top managers in project client organizations should let or even encourage project management practitioners to define the scope of the desired project result in a far-sighted manner. It is the starting point, the basis, for the entire project process, thus, it is a decisive success factor. On the other hand, the attitude of a client organization toward the appropriate use of project implementation strategy (contracting out projects) is also decisive. The client is the primary stakeholder who determines—moreover, creates—the conditions under which an external project is implemented. External contributors need to adapt themselves to these conditions, otherwise there is no potential for them to get the work. Thus, top managers in client organizations should let—moreover, encourage—project managers to formulate appropriate project implementation strategy. It is also time well spent and can be a decisive success factor.

Mihály Görög

Introduction

Nowadays it is broadly accepted by academics and practitioners that projects are the building blocks in implementing organizational strategic objectives. Many articles and books are devoted to highlighting the relationships between strategic objectives and projects. In most of them, however, the authors highlight the relationships between the two, but they do not go into detail. That is, they do not address how to ensure the compliance between a project and its underlying strategic objective. More specifically, the authors do not address how to translate a strategic objective into a manageable project task.

At the same time, the prevailing legal approach, both in literature and practice, characteristic to contracting out projects is considered to be a certain kind of hindrance from the point of view of the context-related use of these tools.

The author of this book is going to address these issues, and also the interrelated questions.

Aims of the Book

The primary aim in writing this book is twofold.

One of the primary aims is to provide an approach and method which facilitates the compliance between a project and its underlying strategic objective throughout the project process. In doing so, the author does not focus on one specific industry or one specific type of project. Instead, different project examples will be used in the book to illustrate the practicability of a strategy-oriented approach when implementing single projects. However, implications for project programs are also considered in this respect.

A strategy-oriented approach to project implementation naturally relies on the role of projects in organizations. Projects are considered to be the building blocks in implementing organizational strategic objectives (i.e., projects are used to implement beneficial changes in organizations). The project result itself is the means by which the required beneficial changes may be accomplished. Therefore, a strategy-oriented approach to project implementation needs to focus, first of all, on the desired project result itself.

Consequently, the above-mentioned primary aim of this book implies:

- Highlighting the role of projects in organizations and introducing both the associated success criteria and the strategy-oriented project cycle.
- Introducing a strategy-oriented scope definition of the desired project result and highlighting the role of the associated feasibility studies to evaluate viability.
- Introducing a strategy-oriented scope control and scope change.
- Introducing a strategy-oriented post-evaluation of the completed project result.

The author is going to provide theoretically based scope management for the desired project result at a practical level. Thus, a certain way of thinking (i.e., approaching the entire issue strategically) is provided.

The other primary aim in writing this book is to provide a systematic way of considering the formulation of appropriate project implementation strategies for external projects. In doing so, the author also does not focus on one specific industry or type of project. In this way, instead of the term contractor, generally the term external contributor or contributor will be used in this book. However, a real estate development project and an information system project will be used in the book to illustrate the use of the toolkit of project implementation strategy. Project implementation strategy, as it is understood in this book, encompasses making decisions on:

- Allocating those responsibilities and risks that are associated with the project triangle during the implementation of the project.
- The use of those tools by means of which a client organization crates competition for potential external contributors.
- Identifying the best bid, based on which projects are awarded to external contributors.

Thus, the above primary aim of the book also implies:

- Introducing the toolkit of project implementation strategy, with special attention paid to clearly differentiating the concept of contract and the concept of payment.
- Highlighting the interrelationships between the tools of project implementation strategy that occur in the course of applying these tools.

Instead of the predominant legal perspective, the author adopts a management perspective that is coupled with the contingency approach in order to avoid the misleading "one problem-one solution" method. The contingency approach is of great importance when making decisions on project implementation strategy (both in a narrow and a broader sense of it).

Scope of the Book

As for the scope, central to this book is the single project, although implications for project programs are also considered in the last chapter of Part I.

As for Part I, this single-project scope of the book is focused on the desired end result of single projects. Due to the role of projects in organizations, it is natural that the project result or more specifically, the scope of the project result is the central focus. However, the author needs to mention some limitations to the scope of Part I. In comparison with publications on project strategy (e.g., Morris and Jamieson 2005), Part I of this book has a rather narrow scope—it is not concerned with the strategic aspects of staffing, scheduling, mitigating risks, etc.

As for Part II, the author needs to mention that traditional approach to contracting out projects is narrow in scope. At the same time, the interrelationships between the tools (contract and payment) and the use of tendering (and the associated prequalification) are neglected in this approach. Based on the adopted management perspective, this book encompasses project implementation strategy in the broadest sense. Thus, this book introduces not only both the types of contracts and the types of payments, but also the types of tendering and the associated prequalification, as well as identifying the best bid. While introducing types of contract and types of payment, emphasis is placed on the inherent characteristics of these tools which constitute the basis of project implementation strategy. Taking into consideration these inherent characteristics makes it possible to make reliable decision on the use of both types of contract and types of payment (i.e., on the project implementation strategy in the narrow sense).

The author also places emphasis on revealing the interrelationships between project implementation strategy in the narrow sense and the use of tendering and that of prequalification. Taking into account these relationships makes it possible to make reliable decisions on project implementation strategy in the broadest sense. Formulating project implementation strategy in the broader sense fosters reliable bid ranking. The latter issue is also covered by this book.

However, the author needs to mention some limitations of Part II as well. This part of the book does not include two emerging project implementation strategy-related issues. These are Public-Private Partnership (PPP) and Build-Own-Operate-Transfer (BOOT) (c.f. Merna and Smith 1994), and partnering (c.f. Alderman and Ivory 2007; Kadefors, Björlingson and Karlsson 2007). Central to the first two phenomena is the involvement of private capital in public projects, while the second one is about improving relationships (in general) between the primary stakeholders of project implementation.

Finally, this book is not a stand-alone comprehensive book, thus the author assumes a basic level of familiarity with the project management concepts.

Structure of the Book

The book comprises two parts, and each part comprises eight chapters. Part I is devoted to a strategy-oriented approach to managing the project result. Part II, considered from a client perspective, is devoted to the phenomenon of strategy for implementing external projects.

Each of the eight chapters in Part I will perform a certain specific task. The first three chapters provide the conceptual and contextual bases for strategy-oriented project implementation, as it is considered in the book. More specifically, Chapter 1 highlights the role of projects in organizations and introduces the interrelationships between projects and strategic objectives. Chapter 2, bearing in mind the role of projects, introduces the success criteria against which the success achieved on projects may be evaluated. This chapter, at the same time, highlights the relationships between success criteria and professional competences, placing emphasis on the role of a strategy-oriented attitude toward projects. Chapter 3 introduces the strategy-oriented project cycle, by means of which both the strategic role of projects and the importance of a strategy-oriented attitude toward the projects may be envisaged.

Chapter 4 is devoted to a strategy-oriented approach and method to defining the scope of the desired project result. In other words, this chapter is concerned with translating a given strategic objective into a project outcome that complies with the underlying strategic objective. Based on this chapter, Chapter 5 introduces the aim of feasibility studies in the course of evaluating the viability of the outlined project idea. At the same time, this chapter highlights the interrelationships between the scope definition and the potential for achieving success on the project. Chapter 6 introduces both strategy-oriented scope control and scope change, and at the same time it discusses the interrelationship between scope definition, scope control, scope change, and the phenomenon of success. Chapter 7 is devoted to introducing a strategy-oriented post-evaluation of the accomplished project result, and highlights the need for subsequent feedback on the scope definition. Finally, Chapter 8 covers the implications for managing project programs. Central to this chapter is the program level use of strategy-oriented scope management. Case examples in this part are used to demonstrate the practicability of the proposed method and approaches.

The eight chapters in Part II also perform specific tasks. Again, the first three chapters provide the conceptual contextual bases, in this case for the phenomenon of project implementation strategy, as it is considered in the book. More specifically, Chapter 1 highlights the concept and the role of project implementation strategy, and identifies the primary stakeholders who play an active role in external projects. Chapter 2 and Chapter 3 introduce the basic types of both contract and payment consecutively. Emphasis is placed on highlighting the inherent characteristics, and on the comparison of the different types of contract and the payment types.

Chapter 4 introduces a systematic approach to formulating project implementation strategy in the narrow sense. This approach is based on matching the previously identified inherent characteristics of both the contract and payment types with the inherent characteristics of both the project and the client. Case examples are also provided in this chapter. Chapter 5 provides an overview on tendering and prequalification, highlighting their role in the context of project implementation strategy in the broader sense. Chapter 6 undertakes to introduce how prequalification needs to be matched with project implementation strategy in the narrow sense. This chapter highlights, at the same time, how the types of contract naturally attract certain types of tender. Case examples illustrate matching tendering and prequalification with the previously formulated project implementation strategy in the narrow sense. Chapter 7 is devoted to bid evaluation, especially to ranking the bids in order to identify the best bid and the best bidder. Bearing in mind the implications of the formulated project implementation strategy in the broader sense, attention is drawn to those factors that determine the appropriate ranking criteria. Finally, Chapter 8 provides a summary of those implied advantages that can be gained by both the client organization and the external contributor when the appropriately formulated project implementation strategy in the broader sense is in use in an external project.

Part I

A Strategy-Oriented Approach To Managing The Project Result

Chapter 1

Strategy and Projects

Taking into account the history of project management, one might say that it was considered first of all in the construction industry until about the middle of the twentieth century. Typical projects aimed at creating different infrastructure facilities, such as buildings, roads, railways, steel structures etc. Then, during the fifties, considerable changes were experienced regarding the use of project management. At that time, this knowledge field began to be used both in the space industry and in the defense industry. In addition, besides traditional construction projects, more and more research and development projects were initiated in many different organizations. At the same time, these circumstances also fostered the development of a project management toolkit.

However, the last twenty years of the twentieth century provided a new path for project management. Fostered by the rapidly growing use of information technology, fast and sometimes chaotic changes became the most decisive features of the operational environment of organizations. A few organizations were able to generate the changes, while others tried to adapt to the changes. This implies that the organizations themselves also had to undergo changes. Due to these circumstances, strategic management (instead of strategic planning) in organizations became of great importance, and strategic management became responsible for providing new vision and the associated goals and objectives for organizations. Accordingly, more and more projects had to be initiated in organizations in order to achieve their strategic objectives. Cleland (1994), who was one of the first to analyze the strategic role of projects and that of project management, states that "Project: management constitutes one of the main forms for converting an organization from one state to another. It might be called *transitional management*."(ibid., 34).

Based on the idea highlighted above, this chapter will briefly introduce the interrelationships between the organizational strategy and projects, while the role of projects in implementing organizational strategy will be emphasized. At the same time, taking into consideration the portfolio of projects in an organization, the author will provide a categorization of projects in order to underpin the primary focus of the book.

Interrelationships Between Strategy and Projects

Broadly speaking, both profit-oriented companies or public service organizations need to carry out certain core activities (e.g., production of predefined products or providing predefined services). The conditions under which the core activities are carried out in an organization are shaped by the internal characteristics of the organization and by the characteristics of its external operational environment. When these characteristics undergo changes, they prompt changes to the conditions of carrying out the core activities. However, these changes may result in new core activities being undertaken by the organization. Therefore, organizations need to face a certain kind of duality. They need to carry out their actual core activities efficiently, while implementing the required changes effectively.

The duality highlighted above, however, implies that managing an organization is a multifaceted phenomenon (Görög 1996; Görög and Smith 1999), that is, it encompasses:

- Strategic management, which defines the future direction of development—the vision—of the organization in order to ensure the survival of the organization itself. It aims at identifying future potential competitive advantages and allocating resources to ensure achieving the vision. Since the external operational environment and also the internal characteristics may change almost continuously, an organization needs to shape and refine the vision and the associated goals and objectives accordingly.
- Project management, which implements the changes implied in the vision and the associated objectives. It aims at implementing the required projects successfully to bring about effective changes.
- Operational management, which ensures that the core activities are carried out not only continuously but efficiently as well. It aims at exploiting the current competitive advantages by means of the actual market position.

These three aspects of managing an organization, however, are strongly interrelated. The ultimate aim of strategic management is to ensure new or improved operational competences for survival. At the same time the direction of change, i.e., identifying the required new or the improved operational competences, is the responsibility of strategic management, while the implementation of these changes is the responsibility of project management. When the desired project result is completed, it starts its operational phase, and in this way, it realizes the change implied in the underlying strategic objective. In other words, projects are considered to be building blocks in implementing organizational strategic objectives (c.f. Cleland 1994).

Besides the strong interrelationships, these three aspects of management show dissimilarities too, and a comparison of them is highlighted in Table 1.1.

Table 1.1 Comparison of management aspects

Aspect of the Comparison	Strategic Management	Project Management	Operational Management
Time horizon of decision-making	Long term	Medium term	Short term
Influence on the organization	Decisive in long term	Decisive in medium term	Decisive in short term
Motivating forces	The likely future operational environment	Beneficial change within predefined cost and time	The actual market and/or the available resources
Nature of the task	Complex and innovative	Complex and innovative	Routine-like and standardized
Continuity of the task	Quasi-continuous	One time but recurring	Continuous
Scope of the task	The entire organization	The entire organization or more than one functional unit	Functional units

Source: Adapted from Görög and Smith (1999, 13)

Nowadays, a bulk of literature is concerned with the role of projects in implementing organizational strategies, for example, Clelend (1994), Morris and Jamieson (2004), Shenhar et al. (2007), just to mention a few. Since most of the readers are familiar with the context of organizational strategy, the author is not going to provide an introduction in detail. However, highlighting the relationship between strategies and projects, and the underlying basic concepts of organizational strategy, is needed to underpin the strategy-oriented approach to managing projects.

One of the most seminal books on organizational strategy was written by Johnson and Scholes (1993). The authors identify the following questions that need to be addressed in the course of developing organizational strategy:

- Based on the likely future operational environment and the internal characteristics of the organization, what is the desired future state of the organization? The answer is given by formulating the appropriate mission and vision for the organization.
- What are the goals and objectives that need to be achieved in order to fulfill the mission, and to achieve the desired future state (the vision)? The answer is given by formulating a general statement of the aims (i.e., the goals), and by means of quantifying these goals when possible, or more precisely formulating them (i.e., the objectives).
- What are the strategies to be undertaken in order to achieve the objectives? The ultimate answer is given by identifying actions by means of which the objectives may be achieved.

The identified actions are such tasks that imply some achievable end results that need to be achieved within a certain time and cost constraint. Thus, each strategic action includes the basic characteristics of a project task (i.e., a predefined end result that need to be achieved on time and at cost). The similarities between strategic actions and projects contributed to identifying the role of projects in implementing strategic objectives. This revelation was first made by Cleland (1990), however around the turn of the century, more and more authors came to the same conclusion (e.g. Görög 1993; van den Honert 1994; McElroy 1996; Grundy 1997; Andersen and Jessen 2003; Leybourne 2007; Kwak and Anbari 2008).

Literature on organizational strategy introduces different strategic options. At the same time, different schools of formulating organizational strategy are also identified in the literature. Introducing these schools and the strategic options available for organizations is beyond the scope of this book. However, we need to note that there are two clear types or two extremes of organizational strategy, while there are a few in-between solutions. One of the clear types is referred to as deliberate strategy, while the other is referred to as emergent strategy. A deliberate strategy is a result of a more formal analysis and planning, while an emergent strategy is the result of a rather spontaneous, flexible process.

This distinction between the two extreme types of strategy implies two different relationships between strategies and projects. In the case of a basically deliberate strategy, one can find a more or less straightforward relationship (i.e., the bespoke strategic objectives will determine the associated projects). However, in the case of a basically emergent strategy, both the strategic objectives and the associated projects evolve parallel to each other, and both the strategic objectives and the projects mutually influence each other.

The Organizational Project Portfolio

Identifying project options is a strategic issue, and it is the responsibility of the project portfolio management. Therefore, each strategic objective needs to be underpinned at least by one project option, otherwise there is no potential for achieving the strategic objective in question. However, it may happen, especially in the case of an emergent strategy, that first some project option emerges, and this option creates the starting point for a certain strategic objective.

When the organizational strategy is formulated in some form or other, it needs to include the associated project options as well. In other words, an organization needs to have a portfolio of projects in order to implement the actual strategic objectives. The previously mentioned interrelationships between the strategic objectives and the associated projects is conceptualized in Figure 1.1.

The double-headed arrows in Figure 1.1 show the potential mutual impact, which is characteristic of the relationships in the situation of a basically emergent strategy.

A project portfolio should encompass all those projects that need to be implemented in an organization in order to achieve the strategic objectives. Thus, the

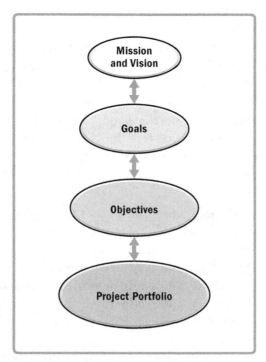

Figure 1.1 Interrelationships between strategy and projects

projects of an organizational project portfolio compete with each other to a certain extent for the organizational resources in the course of their implementation (Archer and Ghasemzadeh 1999). At the same time, there could be changes as to the priority of the strategic objectives in the course of implementing the project portfolio, and these changes could lead to reconsidering the importance of the projects in the portfolio of the organization (Müller, Martinsuo, and Blomquist 2008).

However, an organizational project portfolio may comprise both single projects and project programs. Those projects in a portfolio which are bound together by means of the common resource pool (resource-related interdependence) and/or by means of scope-related interdependence are considered to be one project program (Görög 2011). However, those projects in an organizational project portfolio that may be implemented without considering the resource use of other projects and/or without considering the actual status of other projects that are also under implementation are referred to as single or individual projects. Generally, an organizational project portfolio comprises both single projects and project programs. However, the two extremes—(i.e., only single projects or only one single project program) may also occur.

The author will focus on single projects throughout the book, although the last chapter provides certain implications for the phenomenon of managing project programs.

Grouping of Projects

Single projects may be grouped in many different ways, depending on the approach adopted by the researchers. Introducing the extant approaches regarding grouping the projects is beyond the scope of this book, however, highlighting the most typical approaches may be useful. Wheelwright and Clark (1992) differentiate the types of projects based on the magnitude of change that is induced by the projects. Wateridge (1999) considers the clarity of definition of the expected project result in order to differentiate project types. At the same time, Turner (2006) identifies types of projects according to the degree of novelty inherent in the projects.

Each of the previously mentioned methods of grouping the projects may be important from the point of view of the future potentials of an organization. If the project portfolio of an organization comprises mainly derivative projects (Wheelwright and Clark 1992), the organization will face a weaker competitive position in the long run, while, the dominance of the breakthrough projects implies a better future market position. When the project portfolio of an organization comprises mainly firmly defined projects (Wateridge 1999) the organization may rely on more formal processes in the course of implementing these projects. However, if the project portfolio is dominated by so-called open projects (i.e., projects without clearly defined outcomes that are negotiable), the organization needs to face contingencies. Turner's (2006) categorization, at the same time, makes it possible to predict the future need for project management professionalism in the organization. Therefore, when the project portfolio comprises mainly strangers (projects that are basically different from the previous ones) and aliens (unlike any earlier projects), the organization needs to possess high level of project management professionalism.

Bearing in mind the main focus of this book, the author suggests a categorization of single projects based on the origin of these projects. Thus, we can differentiate projects as follows:

- strategic project,
- problem-solving project,
- event project.

Grundy and Brown (2002) consider a project to be a strategic project only if it has a considerable impact on the entire organization because of the magnitude of change induced by the project itself. The author of this book, however, does not make a distinction between projects based on the magnitude of change. Each project is considered to be a strategic project, independent of the magnitude of the implied change, if the need for the project in question is derived from the strategy of an organization. However, the underlying strategic objective of the project may be based on either a deliberate strategy or an emergent strategy.

At the same time, problem-solving projects are those projects that aim at getting rid of some operational problem (e.g., shortening the process of moving raw materials) or being in compliance with some new legislation and with other expectations (Harris 2009). In the case of a problem-solving project, normally the need for change is not derived from the strategy of the organization. The tasks from this type of project not only include the main features of a project in terms of the project triangle, but they may require a temporary organization as well.

Event projects are also common to many organizations, although these projects do not directly originate from the organizational strategy. A good case in point may be a professional association where the organization of the annual conference is delegated to a different member institution every year. Organizing this event is also considered to be a project both in terms of the project triangle and that of the required temporary organization. Moreover, event projects are generally characterized by a fixed timeframe.

Because of its focus, one of the central themes of this book is strategy-oriented scope definition of a desired project result. To achieve this aim, we should differentiate projects from the point of view of their origin in an organization. Although the emphasis is placed on strategic projects, the method of strategy-oriented scope definition of a desired project result may be applied in the case of other projects as well.

Chapter 2

Success Criteria and Project Management Competences

The previous chapter pointed out the role of projects in organizations. It could be seen that projects are the tools of implementing organizational strategic objectives, while these strategic objectives imply changes. Because of the permanent changes characteristic of the operational environment, appropriate changes of the organizations themselves are of great importance. The direction of the organizational changes is set by the organizational strategy, although the implied changes are implemented by means of projects.

These relationships further imply that projects need to be successfully completed. In other words, the long-term success of an organization relies on successful projects. Thus, interpreting the phenomenon of project success is a salient issue. Statistics say that roughly 20% of the world GDP was spent on projects in 2005 (World Bank 2005); however, according to the well-known CHAOS Report (Standish Group 2009), roughly 60% of the IT/IS projects are considered to be a failure.

Over the last few decades, we have experienced a considerable evolution in the concept of, and the approach to, the phenomenon of project success. Understanding the success achieved by projects is determined by the role of the projects in the organization. On the other hand, an appropriate approach to the phenomenon of project success may direct our attention to the importance of the appropriate scope definition of the desired project result.

This chapter firstly introduces the evolution of an approach to the concept of project success in order to provide a basis for a better understanding of the hierarchical approach to the phenomenon of project success highlighted in the second section of the chapter. Finally, the last section points out how project management competences contribute to achieving success on projects.

Evolution of the Approach to Project Success

The traditional approach to interpreting project success is rooted in the traditional approach to projects. This means that a project is a triangle, that is, a complex task that aims at creating a predefined result within predefined time and cost constraints. Consequently, success achieved on projects was also interpreted based on this triangle. In this way, if the desired project result was completed according to the quality requirements, and on time and to budget, the project was considered to be successful. At the same time, the triangle (quality, time, cost/budget) also was used to assess the success of project management. That is, if the project was completed in accordance with the predefined triangle, the project management was also successful.

Although the traditional approach is narrow in scope, it was appropriate decades ago when the operational environment of organizations underwent changes slowly and gradually. Under these conditions, organizations could develop long-term strategic plans that provided firm bases for the associated projects. There was, therefore, potential for defining properly the desired project result (including the quality requirements), and both the duration time and the cost of implementation (i.e., the project triangle). In other words, there was no potential for unforeseen serious changes in the course of the implementation. Consequently, the predefined project triangle seemed to be a firm ground for evaluating both project success and project management success.

As highlighted in the previous chapter, during the last twenty years of the twentieth century change became the most decisive feature of the operational environment of the organizations. The rapid and occasionally chaotic changes of the operational environment brought into being the phenomenon of strategic management, that is, the need for a quasi-continuous consideration of the future of the organization. Under these conditions, instead of elaborating long-term strategic plans, organizations need to maneuver according to the changing environment. It implies that projects in the course of implementation should also be changed—sometimes cancelled—in order to keep them in line with the actual strategic objectives of the organization.

At the same time, also due to the challenging operational environment, organizations have to reengineer their operational process and their management structure. These efforts resulted in the proliferation of organizational development projects and their associated information system projects. In contrast to the previous predominance of hard projects, these projects are soft in nature. In other words, the desired project result could be defined neither in a quantitative manner nor in detail in advance in the case of these kinds of projects.

Due to the circumstances highlighted above, the project triangle became insufficient as the only success criterion for evaluating the success achieved on projects. Therefore, considerable research efforts were devoted to identifying appropriate success criteria based on which both project success and project management success may be evaluated. One of the milestones of these research efforts was the clear differentiation of the phenomena of success factors and success criteria (Belassi and Tukel 1996). Accordingly, success factors are those conditions and measures that may be influenced to contribute to achieving success, whereas success criteria are those values that need to be met by the project, or those objectives that need to be achieved from the project (Cooke-Davies 2002; Bredillet 2008).

The research outcomes regarding success criteria, based on the underlying research approach, may be grouped into two categories. One of them is referred to as the multi-criteria approach, while the other one is referred to as the value-based approach.

The multi-criteria approach has two common features:

- The project triangle alone is not sufficient; however, it is one of the required criteria to evaluate the success achieved on projects.
- The concept of project management success and project success are different, thus each of them should be evaluated according to a different set of criteria.

Besides the above similarities, there are considerable differences amongst different researchers both in terms of the number of criteria and the criteria needed to evaluate project management success. De Wit (1988) and Cooke-Davies (2002) find that the traditional project triangle is a sufficient criterion against which project management success may be reliably evaluated. At the same time, Baccarini (1999) argues for other criteria besides the triangle to evaluate project management success. He suggests that the quality of the project management process and the satisfaction of those who are involved in the project should be considered as success criteria.

As for the success of the project, contribution to the organizational strategic objectives (Atkinson 1999; Baccarini 1999; Cooke-Davies 2002; Wateridge 1997) and satisfaction of the stakeholders' expectations (Cooke-Davies 2002; De Wit 1988) are suggested as success criteria.

The number of success criteria may vary from author to author, although the reason for this is the different level of detail adopted by the authors.

Taking into account the research outcomes summarized above, one may come to the conclusion that each of the cited authors stresses the need for the following criteria to evaluate both the project management success and project success:

- the project triangle (quality, time, cost),
- contribution to the organizational objectives,
- stakeholder acceptance.

Therefore, the suggested set of success criteria encompasses both quantitative and qualitative criteria. The use of qualitative criteria in particular implies that evaluating the success achieved on projects goes beyond the implementation phase of the project. Stakeholder acceptance, for example, typically might be evaluated during the operational phase of the completed project result (Jugdev and Müller 2005), while the use of a multi-criteria approach may result in conflicting outcomes as to the question of success.

The criticism implied in the last statement leads to the emergence of *the value-based approach* to the question of project success. This approach aims at interpreting the success achieved on projects in terms of monetary value. First Freeman and Beale (1992), then Gardiner and Stewart (2000) introduced a method which utilized the post calculated net present value (NPV) to express the success achieved on projects. Yu, Flett, and Bowers (2005) introduced two value-based measurements to evaluate project success. These are the net project execution cost (NPEC) and the net product operation value (NPOV). Thus, a project is considered to be successful if NPOV > NPEC.

Both the approaches seem to be novel, however, each of them has a narrow outlook at least for two reasons. On the one hand, these approaches consider only the direct financial aspects of a project only from the point view of the investor. However, as highlighted earlier, there are other, equally important considerations. The earlier cited literature provides many examples for project failure due to neglecting stakeholders, for instance. On the other hand, a project manager could influence neither the post-calculated value of NPV nor the post-calculated value of NPOV. Because of the narrow outlook characteristic of the value-based approach to success, the author will not consider this approach in this book.

Hierarchical Approach to Project Success

Taking into consideration the multi-criteria approach to interpreting the success achieved on projects, the following features may be identified of this approach:

- This approach did not conceptually underpin the identified criteria, nor did it define the concept of project success.
- This approach identified the most decisive success criteria, however, this approach did not reveal the interrelationships between the criteria.
- This approach did not address the issue of the relative priority of the different criteria.

The author's research into project success addressed the above issues, while a hierarchical approach to the phenomenon of project success was interpreted. As a conceptual basis for the success of projects, we need to consider the role of projects in organizations. Chapter 1 introduced the role of projects. Accordingly, projects are the means of implementing change implied in the organizational strategic objectives. Therefore, from the point of view of the long-term success of organizations, their projects need to be successful. Taking into consideration this axiomatic assertion, the concept of project success is defined as follows: ***A project may be considered to be successful if the outcome of the project—the project result—contributes to achieving its underlying strategic objective in the organization, and, at the same time, both the implementation process of the project and the***

project result itself are accepted by the stakeholders. This definition directly encompasses both contribution to the organizational objectives and stakeholder acceptance identified by previous research, and it includes the traditional project triangle as well. The potential of the project's result to contribute to the underlying strategic objective may be determined by the actual project triangle to a certain extent as well. Therefore, the above definition implies the following success criteria:

- The traditional project triangle (i.e., implementation cost, implementation time, and quality of the completed project result)
- Client satisfaction (i.e., the potential of the completed project result for achieving its underlying strategic objective)
- Stakeholder satisfaction (i.e., stakeholders' readiness to accept both the implementation process of the project and the project result itself)

Actually, the project client is one of the stakeholders, although we need to consider this player separately. This is justified by the role of the client. While the other stakeholders generally have a passive role (react to the project), the client needs to adopt an active role (i.e., active) in the project.

The multi-criteria approach to project success distinguishes project management success from the success of the project result (e.g., Baccarini 1999). However, these two areas may be interrelated. That is, successful project management may contribute to the success of the project result, although it could not prevent the failure of the project result. On the other hand, the success of the project result may justify the success of project management. This mutual relationship implies that project success is a multi-faceted phenomenon. It implies both the efficiency aspect and the question of effectiveness (c.f. Jugdev and Müller 2005). The efficiency aspect relates to the implementation of the project, while the effectiveness is understood as the impact of the project result. The efficiency of implementing the project is evaluated by means of the project triangle, while effectiveness of the project result is evaluated by means of the client and stakeholder satisfaction.

As pointed out in the previous paragraph, efficiency (management of the project) and effectiveness (impact of the project result) may be interrelated. Therefore, the associated success criteria are also interrelated. This perception leads us to the notion of the hierarchical approach to project success. Accordingly, the previously identified success criteria are interrelated in the following way:

- The project triangle as the lowest-level success criterion makes it possible to measure the success of project management. Since the desired project result may undergo changes during implementation, consequently the predefined values of the triangle may also change. Therefore, the evaluation should be carried out against the actual values of the triangle. Research outcomes of the author (Görög 2001) show that success at this level fosters both client and stakeholder satisfaction. Timely and good quality completion fosters achieving the underlying strategic objective, while completion at cost increases the potential for a favorable financial return. All in all, success in terms of the triangle provides the potential for realizing more benefit in the client organization, which may lead to a higher level of client satisfaction. However, the opposite situation is also true. Lower quality coupled with both cost and time overrun lessens the potential for realizing the expected benefit, thus lessening the potential for client satisfaction. The previous train of thought may also be interpreted in connection with stakeholder satisfaction.

- Client satisfaction as the second level success criterion also implies a two-directional interrelationship. A successful project result that contributes to achieving the underlying strategic objective may qualify the project management process as a success, despite the serious time and cost overrun. At the same time, a successful project result may lead to stakeholder satisfaction, as well (see, e.g., the Sydney Opera House, the London Thames Barrier etc.). However, both the unsatisfied client and stakeholders may undervalue the efficiency of managing the project.

- Stakeholder satisfaction as the third level success criterion may have a considerable impact on the realizable success at the previous levels. Hostile stakeholders emerging in the operational phase of the completed project result may eliminate the potential for client satisfaction, and also may undervalue the efficiency of managing the project (see, e.g., the Budaörs Logistics Centre of the National Post of Hungary). One might say that the operation was a success but the patient died. However, supportive stakeholder attitude may result in client satisfaction which can leverage the perceived efficiency of managing the project.

The hierarchic order of the success criteria may be comprehended based on the interrelationships existing between them. Hence, the lowest level success criterion is the triangle, which is followed by the client satisfaction, and finally, stakeholder satisfaction is on the top. The highlighted interrelationships imply that a higher-level success criterion includes—at least indirectly—the requirements of the lower-level success criterion. This approach to the project success implies the following possibilities:

- Different players and stakeholders of the project may evaluate the success achieved on the project at the appropriate level, that is, against the adequate criterion (e.g., the project team or the external contributors against the project triangle, the sponsor in terms of the client satisfaction, and so forth)
- The client organization, based on the underlying strategic objective, may determine the relative importance of the success criteria in advance which will be considered:
  - in the course of defining the desired project result
  - in the course of controlling the project implementation
  - in the course of initiating change during the implementation

The success criteria encompassed by this approach are in line with the definition of project success given in this section, while the considered criteria make it possible to evaluate both the efficiency and the effectiveness of the project. While the efficiency may be evaluated when the project is completed, the effectiveness generally could be evaluated reliably during the operational phase of the project result (Jaafari 2007; Turner 2004). It is especially true when decisive stakeholders are found in the operational phase.

The following case examples provide a better understanding of the hierarchical approach to project success.

- A company that operated in the hotel industry wanted to penetrate the conference tourism segment of the market. To achieve this objective, a project was initiated that aimed at constructing a new hotel building. The client, taking into consideration the actual demand of the market, defined the desired project result and the associated time and cost constraints. However, in the course of implementing the project, the client realized the changing demand of the market but, in order to avoid time and cost overrun, the client was reluctant to initiate the required changes in the desired project result. Therefore, the project was completed in accordance with its original definition (project triangle). Because of the changing market demand, the use rate of the hotel building was below 30% during the first few years of its operation.

  Although, the project was a success in terms of the project triangle, it was a failure in terms of client satisfaction; however, there were no hostile stakeholders. Due to the failure to implement changes, the completed hotel building could not contribute to achieving the underlying strategic objective. The lack of client satisfaction finally eliminated the perceived project management success.

- A commercial bank at the beginning of the 1990s initiated an information system project in order to attract more customers by means of reducing the time period needed for transactions. The project was completed according to the predefined project triangle, and the completed system was taken into operation to the client's satisfaction. However, in the course of operation, the end users of the system (the employees of the bank) were reluctant to use it, since they were not prepared in advance for a different way of working. Moreover, they exaggerated the initial operational problems and communicated them to the customers. Consequently, many customers left the bank.

  The project seemed to be a success both in terms of the project triangle and the client satisfaction, however, both these potentials became eliminated because of the hostile attitude of the internal stakeholders.

- A car dealer organization, in order to increase its market share, decided to open a new showroom. To achieve this objective, an appropriate building complex needed to be completed. The construction project was completed to the predefined quality, however, serious time and cost overrun was experienced in the project. Because of the properly aligned marketing part of the entire project, the client achieved an increase in the market share, as expected, during the first year of operation. At the same time, the project did not attract hostile stakeholders.

Since the underlying strategic objective was realized, the client was satisfied with the project result. Thus, the perceived project management success was enhanced and finally it was recognized because of client satisfaction.

The above case examples, at the same time, highlight the importance of both the quantitative and qualitative criteria (Aubry, Hobbs, and Thuillier 2007).

Matching Competences with Success—The Role of a Project Management Toolkit

Undertaking research into project success, Atkinson (1999) identified two types of errors. Type I occurs when something is done wrong (e.g., poor planning, inappropriate estimation, etc.), while Type II emerges when something is forgotten or not done as appropriately as it could be done. What is behind the errors in project management is the lack or the inappropriate utilization of project management competences. Gido and Clements (1999) also emphasize that professionalism allows the project result to be created; however, a project management toolkit is needed for the professionals. All in all, knowledgeable people are considered to be the most important success factor.

The author's research (Görög 2007) into project success revealed certain relationships between a project management toolkit and success criteria in the context of project management competence. As to the aspects of competence in project management we can differentiate technical aspects, human aspects, and project aspects. From the point of view of highlighting the relationships between a project management toolkit and success criteria, only the project aspect needs to be considered. Since the project management practitioner is the focus, at the same time we rely on a competent input approach (c.f. Alam et al. 2008). This approach assumes that people need to have knowledge, skill, and attitude to be competent at project work (Cleland 1994).

In a project context, bearing in mind only the project aspect of competence, the competence comprises of:

- Knowledge, which implies the familiarity with the project management toolkit.
- Skill, which implies the ability to use the knowledge.
- Attitude, which implies the approach toward both projects and managing projects.

Skill presumes knowledge, that is, what we do not know we cannot use. Thus, knowledge and familiarity with the project management toolkit is of great importance to achieve success on projects. The project management toolkit comprises two kinds of tools:

- Quantitative tools, by means of which the quantitative aspects of the projects (e.g., time planning, cost estimation, risk assessment, control, etc.) may be managed
- Qualitative tools, by means of which the qualitative aspects of the projects (e.g., definition of the project result, coordination of implementation, achieving stakeholder acceptance, etc.) may be managed

Project management methodologies are not considered here, since these are rather formalized processes that regulate the steps, and the associated players and documents.

Earlier research undertaken by the author (Görög 2001) found that the majority of project managers were familiar with only quantitative project management tools Although most of the literature (e.g., Fortune and White 2006) points out that success or failure is rooted back to mainly qualitative issues (e.g., weak scope definition, improper coordination, etc.). Although it is common that most failed projects suffer from both time and cost overrun, these overruns are only the symptoms (Type I errors) of the underlying root reasons (Type II errors), such as weak scope definition, unsatisfied stakeholders, etc. Neither cost estimation nor time scheduling could be reliable without a firm starting point (e.g., clear scope definition).

Therefore, we may conclude that the following relationships exist between the project management toolkit and the success criteria. The quantitative tools may contribute to achieving success in terms of the project triangle. At the same time, the qualitative tools may contribute to achieving success in terms of both client and stakeholder satisfaction. Table 2.1 further details these relationships. However, the qualitative tools need to be used properly in order to provide a reliable basis and support for using the quantitative toolkit.

The attitude, that is, the approach to projects and project management need to be strategy-oriented. This kind of approach is required because of the role of projects in the organization, since projects are building blocks in implementing the changes implied in the strategic objectives. A strategy-oriented approach necessitates:

- Defining the scope of the desired project result in compliance with the underlying strategic objective;
- Initiating changes regarding the project result under implementation when the underlying strategic objective or other environmental factors undergo change; and
- Implementing the required change regarding the project result in line with the changing strategic objective or with the changing environmental factors.

Table 2.1 Relationships between PM toolkit and the success criteria

Project Management Tools	Success Criteria

Quantitative tools
    Time planning, resource
    allocation, and cost estimation
 	
    Risk assessment
 	
    Process control
    (earned value analysis)
	The project triangle

Qualitative tools
    Scope definition
 	
    Feasibility studies
 	
    Project organizations
 	
    Project implementation strategy
 	
    Scope control
	Client satisfaction

Stakeholder analysis Project marketing	Stakeholder satisfaction

Although people are the key factor for achieving success on projects, the key tool for these professionals is the strategy-oriented scope definition and change management, and the associated scope control of the desired project result.

Obscure scope definition eliminates the potential for project success in terms of each criterion, since:

- Obscure scope definition does not tend to result in compliance with the underlying strategic objective. Consequently, it is not likely to make strategy-oriented scope control and change management possible. Finally, it should not lead to client satisfaction.
- Obscure scope definition does not tend to make it possible to identify stakeholders reliably. Consequently, it does not usually make effective stakeholder management possible. Finally, it may not lead to stakeholder satisfaction.
- Obscure scope definition does not tend to make it possible to identify the project tasks (activities) to be completed. Consequently, it will not usually result in reliable cost estimation and time planning. Finally, it may lead to both cost and time overrun.

Thus, in order to ensure potential for achieving success on projects strategy-oriented scope management (i.e. definition, control, and change) is a very important key competence for project management professionals. In other words, since the associated project management tools are not panaceas, knowledgeable people are needed to achieve success (Besner and Hobbs 2008).

Chapter 3

The Strategy-Oriented Project Cycle

The previous chapter, among others, highlighted the decisive role of a strategy-oriented approach toward projects and to managing projects. Chapter 1, at the same time, emphasized the uniqueness of each project, and pointed out the diversity of projects. Thus, one could say that each project implies a unique process in the course of its implementation. Consequently, there is no potential for conceptualizing the project process in one single figure.

The above conclusion seems to be true when we approach this issue at the level of each single project. However, applying a higher level of abstraction may help to reveal those features of the project process that are common to any project. By considering the common features of the project process, one can develop the general idea of this process which results in the concept of project cycle. The project cycle is a conceptual framework of the project process (Görög and Smith 1999). The project cycle encompasses those phases of the project process that are common to each project, and highlight those main tasks that are encapsulated in the different phases.

This chapter focuses on introducing a strategy-oriented model of the project cycle. Despite the inevitably strong interrelationship between the existence of projects and the organizational strategic objectives, the extant literature continues in the traditional way with this theme. For the sake of better understanding the relevance of a strategy-oriented concept of the project cycle, firstly the most characteristic extant views on the project cycle will be introduced. This will be followed by introducing a strategy-oriented conceptualization of the project cycle. The last section of this chapter is devoted to summarizing the most important implications of the strategy-oriented approach to the project cycle.

Extant Views on the Project Cycle

One of the earliest definitions of a project cycle is given by Cleland and King (1975). Accordingly, the project cycle represents the "natural and pervasive order of thought and action" (ibid., 186) in order to provide a standardized concept of the consecutive phases of projects. Based on an extensive literature review, Bonnal, De Jonghe, and Ferguson (2002) identified the following approaches toward a project cycle:

- straightforward project cycle,
- control-oriented project cycle,
- quality-oriented project cycle,
- risk-oriented project cycle,
- fractal project cycle.

Both the straightforward model and the fractal model are linear in nature, since each of them depicts the project process against time. However, the fractal approach comprises more phases in order to better fit in the projects with high uncertainty. At the same time, the other three approaches, as additional tools, may contribute to better achieving the aim implied in their name. Hence, the straightforward, that is, the linear approach, is considered to be the most widely accepted approach nowadays. However, different authors identify a different number of phases of the project cycle, while the denomination of the phases may be also different.

The most popular linear approach (Cleland 1994; Pinto and Prescott 1990) differentiates four phases of the project cycle. Figure 3.1 visualizes these phases, while the tasks of a new product development project are indicated for each phase.

Turner (1999) also differentiates four phases of the cycle, however, these are named as germination (proposal and initiation), growth (design and appraisal), maturity (execution and control), and metamorphosis (finalization and closeout). Similarly to the previous approaches, Gido and Clements (1999) identify four phases (need identification, solution development, project performance, and project termination). These phases are also depicted against time and in terms of the effort needed to complete them. However, the level of effort in this concept is asymmetrical, which has its peak before the end of the third phase. On the other hand, the authors also consider the tasks associated with bidding (in the case of external projects) amongst the project tasks.

Jugdev and Müller (2005) provide a general model of the project cycle and different industry-specific versions of the general model as well. However, their general model of the project cycle resembles that of Gido and Clements (1999). An overview of these models is encapsulated in Table 3.1.

A Guide to the Project Management Body of Knowledge (PMBOK® Guide) (Project Management Institute 2008) also proposes a general model of the project cycle which comprises phases and the associated project management process groups. The *PMBOK® Guide* project cycle includes:

- Initiating,
- Planning,

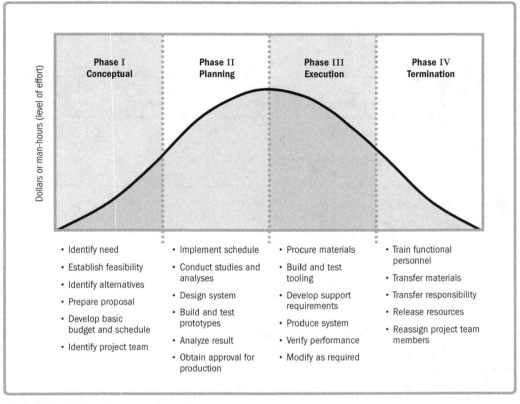

Figure 3.1 Cleland's project cycle
Source: Cleland (1994, 47)

Table 3.1 Different project cycles provided by Jugdev and Müller

Project Phases in the General Model	Construction Industry	Pharmaceutical Industry	Defence Acquisition	Software Development
Initial phase (conceptualization and planning)	Feasibility	Discovery and screening	Concept exploration and definition	Proof of concept cycle
Intermediate phase(s) (production and/or implementation)	Planning and design	Pre-clinical development	Demonstration and validation	First build cycle
	Production	Registration(s) workup	Engineering and manufacturing development	Second build cycle
Final phase (handing over)	Turnover and start up	Post-submission activity	Production and deployment	Final cycle including testing
				Final build

Source: Adapted from Jugdev and Müller (2005, 22)

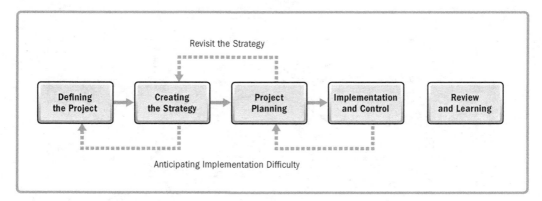

Figure 3.2 The strategic project process
Source: Grundy and Brown (2002, 13)

- Executing,
- Monitoring and Controlling,
- Closing.

Bearing in mind those projects that deliver organizational breakthroughs, Grundy and Brown (2002) developed the strategic project process which is conceptualized in the following cycle (Figure 3.2).

In comparison with the linear models of the project cycle, this idea is different. The authors take into consideration the potential iterations between the phases, however; the phases in their model are referred to as stages.

Strategy-Oriented Approach to the Project Cycle

Nowadays, it is broadly accepted by both academics and practitioners that projects are means of achieving changes implied in the organizational strategic objectives. The inevitable strategy-oriented approach to projects and project management is considered to be of great importance. It seems to be a strange paradox, then, that the academic community goes on applying the traditional linear project cycle. The most significant drawbacks of this approach are as follows:

- It does not reveal the relationships between projects and their underlying strategic objectives, since it assumes that projects are externally given for the project team
- It relies on a linear way of thinking, assuming that a project is a straightforward process that does not imply the potential for change

However, projects are born of strategies, and nowadays they inevitably undergo changes during their life cycle. Developing a strategy-oriented project cycle

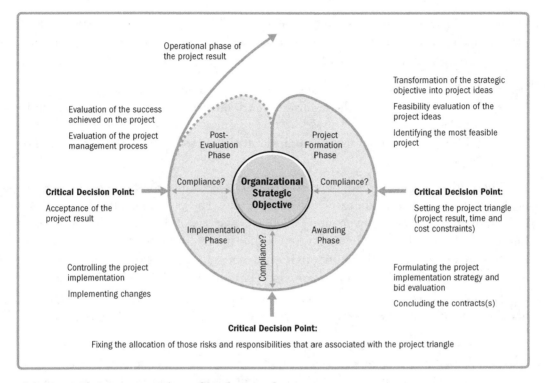

Figure 3.3 The strategy-oriented project cycle
Source: Adapted from Görög and Smith (1999, 20)

is an answer to this challenge. A strategy-oriented project cycle is a circle-like framework, according to which the project tasks move around a hub. The hub itself is the underlying strategic objective of the given project. This type of project cycle is conceptualized in Figure 3.3, and it was introduced first by the author of this book.

The strategy-oriented project cycle—also taking into account the tasks undertaken in an external project—implies four phases of the project, namely:

- project formation,
- awarding,
- implementation,
- post-evaluation.

A strategy-oriented project cycle reveals the critical decision points of the project process, while these critical decision points mark off the phases of the cycle. At the same time, the importance of the critical decision points needs to be considered from the point of view of the underlying strategic objective as well. This latter relationship is highlighted by means of the double-headed arrows between each critical decision point and the strategic objective in the hub of the cycle. The critical decision points consecutively imply:

- Making a decision on the project triangle based on the feasibility studies
- Making a decision on the external contributor(s), and on the contract(s) to be included; and
- Making a decision on the acceptance of the (completed) project result, and on the project closer.

The critical decision points are referred to as critical points due to the impacts of the decisions made at these points of the cycle. The outcomes of these decisions reduce the flexibility of implementing changes. The use of the double-headed arrows highlights the need for evaluating whether the actual status of the desired project result is in compliance with its underlying strategic objective before making decisions at critical points. This is much easier to do before the critical decision than after it.

However, the so-called borders between the phases in the strategy-oriented project cycle should not be viewed as fixed marks, at least for the following reasons:

- There may be overlaps between the phases for two main reasons:
  - Especially in the case of soft projects (e.g., organizational development projects and the associated information system projects), there is no potential for defining the desired project result in appropriate detail until the end of the first phase of the cycle. Details of the desired project result, however, will be defined at the milestone events of the implementation phase.
  - Especially in the case of external projects (e.g., real estate development projects) when there are a few external contributors (traditional type of contract), the awarding phase may overlap with the implementation phase. Thus, tendering and bidding and bid evaluation also may occur in the implementation phase, while several external contributors are working on different work packages.
- There may be a need for evaluating compliance more frequently than at the highlighted critical decision points when they occur in the cycle. The previous two cases (soft projects and the use of traditional type of contract) are good cases in point. On the other hand, especially in the case of novel research and development projects, there may be ramifications in the course of the development process. The ramifications require decisions, which, in turn, require the evaluation of compliance in the course of implementation as well.

Although Figure 3.3 points out the main project management tasks encompassed in the project phases, a brief summary of them is provided here:

The project formation phase needs to focus on, based on the underlying strategic objective, defining the scope of the achievable project result in terms of project ideas (see Chapter 4). Then the viability of the ideas is evaluated by means of feasibility studies to identify the most viable project idea (see Chapter 5). This phase of the project cycle results in making a decision on the project triangle. Thus, the outcome of the first phase will determine the tasks of the following phases to a great extent.

The awarding phase is also a decisive phase, although it is needed only in the case of external projects. First, the project implementation strategy (type of contract and type of payment) needs to be formulated. Then the appropriate type of tendering and the potentially associated prequalification is decided. These tasks form the bases for proceeding with tendering and bid evaluation to conclude contract(s).

The implementation phase requires both process control and scope control to form the bases of initiating and implementing both corrections and changes if needed (see Chapter 6). The implementation phase results in the completed project result, and in accepting and taking it into operation. This phase ends with a project closer.

The post-evaluation phase is part of the operational phase of the completed project result, and generally has a twofold aim. On the one hand, the evaluation of success achieved on the project is undertaken in order to reveal the potential for achieving the underlying strategic objective (see Chapter 7). While on the other hand, the evaluation of the project management process is considered. The latter is wisely imbedded in the organizational learning process.

The entire cycle takes its starting point from a certain strategic objective, although it may also take a direction toward the organizational strategy in the last phase. A completed project may generate further strategic objectives in the project owner organization.

Relevancy of the Strategy-Oriented Project Cycle

Projects, from the point of view of the extent to which a desired project result may be quantified, are grouped into two broad categories, namely hard (with well-defined outcomes) and soft (outcomes are not predefined clearly) projects (see, e.g., Neal 1995; Atkinson, Crawford and Ward 2006). Between these two extremes there may be many in-between cases, although nowadays an increasing number of soft projects is experienced. At the same time, novel projects—due to their novelty itself—imply a number of unforeseeable ramifications as to how to proceed to get the desired project result. Finally, the underlying strategic objective may undergo changes in the course of implementing the project, although these features are amalgamated in a single project in many cases. Even if one of the previously mentioned alternatives occurs in a project, project managers need to face the following issues:

- Potential for inaccurate scope definition of the desired project result.
- Potential for unforeseeable changes in the course of implementing the project.

- Potential for unforeseeable decisions that need to be made in the course of implementing the project either because of the inaccurate scope definition or because of the unforeseeable changes.

Each of these issues may result in such a completed project result that is different from the one that was desired—that is, project failure. In order to eliminate or at least minimize the potential for any non-intentional deviation, project managers need to adopt a strategy-oriented approach not only to the projects but to managing the projects as well. A strategy-oriented project cycle is one of the tools that provides a basis to achieve this end.

Inaccurate scope definition of the desired project result does not necessarily mean inadequate and vague definition of the project result. It means, first of all, that there is no way to predefine the desired project result in detail due to the nature of the project. It implies that the project result needs to be defined in fine detail during the implementation phase.

Unforeseeable changes may occur due to the changes in the underlying strategic objective or to the changing operational environment (e.g., changing customer expectations). It implies that the project result needs to be redefined (maybe several times) during the implementation phase.

The need for (re)defining the project result more precisely may emerge in the awarding phase too, in the case of an external project. However, whenever this need emerges, it requires a similar management response, that is, a strategy-oriented decision-making. Both defining the project result more precisely (in detail) and redefining it necessitate the evaluation of compliance. Decisions made in these situations should result in a project result that is in compliance with the actual status of its underlying strategic objective.

To address these needs, a strategy-oriented project cycle highlights the necessity of:

- A strategy-oriented scope definition of the desired project result (however, this may not always be satisfied in detail); and
- A strategy-oriented approach to managing the project throughout its life cycle.

Experience proves that when the strategy orientation in the project cycle is neglected, contributors (both internal and external) may successfully influence the decisions made by the owner organization according to their own interest. Thus, the contributors, because of their usual solutions, or based on other advantages, are able to draw the project result away from the owner's interest, that is, from the underlying strategic objective. The following chapters—as indicated earlier—further discuss the implications of a strategy-oriented approach.

Chapter 4

The Strategy-Oriented Project Scope Definition

Chapter 1 introduced the role of projects in organizations. Accordingly, projects are a means of realizing strategic objectives, thus projects should deliver some beneficial changes implied in the organizational strategy. Thus organizations need to achieve success on their projects, otherwise there is no potential for successful survival and long-term success.

Chapter 2 introduced those success criteria based on which the success achieved on projects may be evaluated. One of these success criteria is client satisfaction, which is based on the extent to which a completed project result contributes to achieving the underlying strategic objective. Achieving client satisfaction, therefore, postulates defining the desired project result in compliance with its underlying strategic objective. At the same time, the authors cited in Chapter 2 (e.g., Fortune and White 2006) also pointed out that one of the most decisive success or failure factors is the appropriateness of defining the desired project result. This circumstance also justifies the need for defining the scope of the desired project result not only clearly but again at the same time in compliance with its underlying strategic objective.

Chapter 3 introduced the strategy-oriented project cycle, and further underpinned the need for a strategy-oriented approach to projects and project management. A strategy-oriented approach is especially needed in the course of defining the desired project result. According to a strategy-oriented project cycle, defining the scope of the desired project result takes place in the first phase (project formation) of the cycle.

Literature on scope definition is limited, while scope definition in practice is rather vague. At the same time, the use of the term scope definition seems to be ambiguous in the extant literature. In certain cases, it means defining the scope of work to be implemented, while in other cases, it means the units of the project result delivered by the project. In this book, the term project scope is understood as the content of the desired project result.

The aim of this chapter is to introduce an approach to defining the desired project result—in terms of the scope of the project result—based on the underlying strategic objective to be achieved by means of the project in question. This approach and the associated method were developed by the author in the course of research into project scope definition (Görög and Smith 1999; Görög 2000; Görög 2011). However, first the extant approaches to project scope definition will be summarized in order to provide evidence for a strategy-oriented project scope definition. Central to the method are strategic projects (see Chapter 1); however, both problem-solving projects and event projects will be considered.

Extant Approaches to Scope Definition

The importance of scope definition of the desired project result derives from the role of projects in organizations and their associated success criteria. However, Cano and Lidón (2011) state that defining the expected project result is a process in which the stakeholder expectations are identified and the associated specifications are defined.

At the same time, the mutual relationship between strategic objectives and projects is a question of interest in many publications. Turner (1999) concludes that management by projects seems to be the way in which organizations realize their business objectives. Turner and Müller (2003, 3) emphasize that organizations adopt projects in order to implement "a coherent set of change objectives." Andersen and Jessen (2003, 457) state that projects are "venues for mastering business and change." Jugdev and Müller (2005) highlight the importance of projects and project management in the course of creating business value, that is, creating competitive advantage. Winter et al. (2006, 644) draw attention to the increasingly important "challenge of linking business strategy to projects" to maximize revenue and benefits for the stakeholders of the organization. Aubry et al. (2007, 332) propose a definition regarding the phenomenon of organizational project management that was articulated "as means to implement corporate objectives through projects in order to maximize value."

The importance of scope definition of the desired project result also derives from the concept of strategic alignment of projects. Gareis (2004) argues that different projects in an organization need to be joined together as a coherent whole. Morris and Jamieson (2005) state that project management at strategic level is the means to implement corporate strategy; in this way, translating strategy into projects is an outstanding core process in an organization. Some authors, for example Kaplan and Norton (2004), emphasize the need for such a project portfolio that is in line with the organizational strategic objectives. Moreover, these authors proposed the use of such maps by means of which match the strategic objectives and the associated projects can be visualized. Matching strategic objectives and projects is of great importance, since if a certain strategic objective is not matched with a project, it means that the strategic objective in question will not be achieved.

Although the question of alignment is conceived at the strategic level of an organization, it is not sufficiently conceived at project level. The need for aligning strategic objectives with projects implies the need for translating strategic objectives into achievable desired project results by means of defining the scope of desired project result. This is the alignment at project level.

Literature on scope definition of the desired project result is limited, or at least vague, although most professionals acknowledge its importance. However, there is no definite tool or method published as to how to do it. At the same time, there is some disagreement as to what is understood by scope definition.

Grundy and Brown (2002) define the scope of the project in a unique manner, that is *project size x duration x interdependencies*. According to the approach of these authors, the size component of the scope means the number of those units of the organization upon which the project makes its impact, and the significance of the impact, and so forth. In the view of Grundy and Brown, the project scope is, to a great extent, the scope of impact of the project.

The *PMBOK® Guide* (Project Management Institute, 2008) devotes a whole chapter to this issue, called "Project Scope Management." This chapter clearly differentiates product scope (i.e., the features and functions of the project result) and project scope (i.e., the work that needs to be completed to deliver the result). The *PMBOK® Guide* also defines processes that involve collecting requirements, defining scope, creating work breakdown structure, verifying scope, and controlling scope. At the same time, this chapter of the *PMBOK® Guide* introduces a set of tools for completing both product and project scope. Gido and Clements (1999, 106) state that the "first step in the planning process is to define the project objective—the expected result or end product." They emphasize the need for specifications and plans that provide the details of the scope. Andersen, Grude, and Haug (2004) introduced the so-called Mission Breakdown Structure by means of which the project goals are outlined. This structure visualizes a certain desired future status of the organization that should be achieved by means of a certain project.

Bonnal et al. (2002) argue for using tree-like structures to define the end product (project result) of the project, and to define the organization and the process that materialize the end product. These authors suggest the following structures: project/product breakdown structures (PBS); functional breakdown structure (FBS); assembly breakdown structure (ABS); organizational breakdown structure (OBS); work breakdown structure (WBS); and cost/contract breakdown structure (CBS). Both PBS and FBS are used to define the scope of the desired project result. The first one (the PBS) "aims to split the final deliverable of the project into systems, then subsystems—down to elementary parts." The second one (the FBS) "is oriented to the functions the final deliverable should satisfy" (Bonnal et al. 2002, 18).

However, in connection with project programs, Thiry (2002), partly based on Görög and Smith (1999), also argues for the use of the function breakdown structure. He states that it is "the framework of the program" since this tool "classifies function/benefit/objectives from the more abstract strategic objective to the more concrete project solution" (Thiry 2002, 225). In this way, it visualizes the functional requirements of a project or a program outcome.

Görög (2000) and Görög and Smith (1999) go beyond the need for functional requirements, and they argue for considering non-functional requirements as well. They visualize these two types of requirements by means of a function-goal structure to provide a basis for the scope of the desired project result.

The authors who are cited in this section of the book also emphasize that a clear and unambiguous scope definition of the desired project result is of great importance from the point of view of achieving project success. Others such as Van Der Merve (2002) state that strategic vision should be converted into performance targets (i.e., projects), while Burgess, Byrne, and Kidd (2003) say that configuration management would be a potential tool in this process. Nevertheless, a practical solution of translating a given strategic objective into a desired project result seems to be lacking, since the above authors did not introduce such an approach or method by means of which one can undertake translating strategy into projects.

Strategy Based Definition of the Desired Project Result— The Strategic Projects

Again, because of the role of projects in organizations and the associated success criteria, there is a need for some approach and method that support defining the scope for the desired project result that is capable of realizing the underlying given strategic objective. Söderholm (2008) highlights that the potential for project success is basically determined by the extent to which the project is in compliance with the underlying strategic objective. At the same time, Anantatmula (2008) points out that transforming strategic objectives into measurable project objectives acts as a motivating factor for the project team.

Organizational strategic objectives imply the required beneficial changes that are to be archived by means of creating project results that have the capabilities to realize these changes. The term beneficial means, in this respect, the potential for survival and success. That is, benefits should be linked to the project output (the project result), as was also emphasized by Bennington and Baccarini (2004). Turner (2006, 2) also states that "projects deliver beneficial change." Yu et al. (2005) point out that a project result might have functions and features, while Thiry (2002) also highlights the central role of functions when defining programs and associated projects. Görög (2000), and Görög and Smith (1999) use the terms functional and non-functional capabilities when defining the scope of the desired project result.

Indeed, any project result, whatever the type of the project, has functional capabilities and non-functional features. These may be commonly referred to as capabilities. Functional capabilities imply operational processes, for example, screening certain data when developing a new mobile phone set, although low-cost productivity or the design of the phone set are non-functional capabilities. Both types of capabilities should be in compliance with the realizable benefits implied in the underlying given strategic objective of the desired project result. In other words, the project result itself should be in compliance with the implied beneficial changes of the underlying strategic objective. The compliance of the desired project result is required not only in terms of the scope of capabilities but in terms of quality and capacity (or size or dimension) as well. Neither quality nor capacity (or size or dimension) stands alone; thus, they should be interpreted in connection with the required capabilities.

Therefore, in order to ensure the above-mentioned strategic compliance in the course of defining the scope of a desired project result to achieve a certain given strategic objective, we need to address the following questions:

- Q #1: *What are the beneficial changes implied in the strategic objective in question, and what is the associated project result as a whole?*
- Q #2: *What are those capabilities of the desired project result by means of which the required beneficial changes can be achieved?*
- Q #3: *What are the quality and capacity (or size or dimension) requirements that should be associated with the capabilities in order to realize the beneficial changes to be achieved?*
- Q #4: *What are those characteristics of the operational environment (natural, organizational, legal etc.) of the expected project result that could have an impact on the operability of the project result itself?*
- Q #5: *What are those capability providers (either tangible or intangible) that, being integrated as one particular project result, can provide the identified capabilities according to the specified quality and capability (or size or dimension) requirements, within the revealed operational environment of the desired project result?*

The above questions are interrelated, and they have an input-output relationship, while there is a potential for several variations as well. The outcomes of addressing Q #1 to Q #3 make it possible to outline the scope of the desired project result in terms of capabilities and the associated capacity and quality requirements. These outcomes may be referred to as the project idea, which may be conceptualized in a *Capability Breakdown Structure* (see Figure 4.1). The use of this term is justified, since the capabilities of the desired project result encompass both functional and non-functional features. Addressing Q #4 makes it possible to address Q #5, which results in the desired project result in its tangible and/or intangible terms. However, these latter issues (Q #4 and Q #5) belong to the question of viability (see Chapter 5).

It may happen, however, that a project idea is elaborated in several versions. These versions may differ from each other in terms of capabilities, and/or in terms of quality and capacity (or size or dimension) requirements.

Case Example

The following example is used to illustrate the practicability of the approach rather than providing a complete project solution.

As one of their strategic objectives, a company that operates in the food industry seeks to increase the market share by means of penetrating a new market with an existing product in a predefined time period, and within a predefined budget. *The implied beneficial changes* (Q #1) to be realized are as follows:

- The product will be accepted and recognized by the potential customers and local business partners
- The product will be accepted by the local health authority

The associated project result (also Q #1) is that the product will have been introduced to the target market.

The capabilities of the desired project result (Q #2), by which the above beneficial changes can be achieved, are as follows:

- Creating customer demand
- Demonstrating reliability for customers
- Demonstrating safety for the health authority
- Highlighting business potential for the local partners
- Providing recognizability of the producer

Figure 4.1 shows the Capability Breakdown Structure of the desired project result.

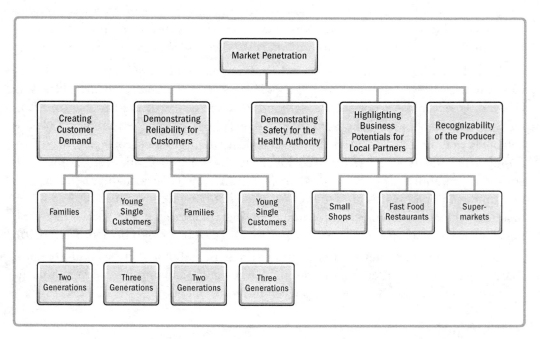

Figure 4.1 The capability breakdown structure of a market penetration project result

To specify both quality and capacity (or size or dimension) requirements associated with the capabilities justifies breaking down the main capabilities into sub-capabilities, then the sub-capabilities into more specific units. Breaking down the main capabilities into smaller units is also justified by the need to identify the decisive characteristics of the operational environment, and to identify the capability providers of the desired project result. When necessary, the capabilities can be broken down into even more basic units. This process could result in, according to Figure 4.1, a different number of breakdown levels in the case of the different main capabilities.

For example, the main capability called "creating customer demand" does not need to be more detailed to specify quality (e.g., according to the code of practice of the local marketing association), and to specify dimension (e.g., 50% of the potential customers). However, this capability should be further detailed in order to reveal the characteristics of the operational environment, such as the cultural differences between "families" and "young single customers," and legislation on advertising, etc. A detailed breakdown is also required in the case of the latter capability ("creating customer demand") in order to specify the most appropriate capability providers (e.g., electronic or printed media, etc.) for each specific customer group, for example, two-generation families (parents and children) and three-generation families (parents and children and grandparents).

Since projects and the project results are different, as are their underlying strategic objectives, there could be very different capabilities for different project results. Thus, a product development project could include, for example, controlling water temperature as a functional capability, and low production cost as a non-functional capability for a washing machine development project. In the case of a house construction project, one of the functional capabilities could be providing the possibility for preparing meals, and one of the non-functional capabilities is the design of the building.

Of course, both the complexity of the desired project result and the clarity of the underlying given strategic objective determine the available capability breakdown structure both in terms of size (e.g., the number of the main capabilities) and details (i.e., the number of breakdown levels). Thus, the process of scope definition could imply multiple variations, while there is a need for flexibility. Olsson (2006) highlights the need for flexibility in the course of scope definition, while Pollack (2007) highlights the potential danger of a premature scope freeze. The dilemma of flexibility versus scope freeze will be discussed further in Chapter 5.

Scope Definition of Non-Strategic Projects

Besides so-called strategic projects, we differentiated problem-solving projects and event projects (see Chapter 1). Bearing in mind the approach and the method when defining the scope of the desired project result in the case of a strategic project, now we turn our attention to defining the scope of non-strategic projects.

Problem-Solving Projects

Projects usually happen at the operational level of organizations in order to remedy an operational problem. In this case, there is no one given a particular and predefined strategic objective behind the project. However, in such a case, the previously outlined approach and method can also be utilized in the course of elaborating the associated project result to be achieved. Similar to a strategic objective, remedying a certain operational problem (e.g., shortening the route of movement of raw materials in a workshop) also implies some beneficial changes. These beneficial changes need to be realized in order to provide a solution for the problem in question. Consequently, only the first of the five questions introduced in the previous section needs to be changed. Thus, in the case of a so-called problem solving project the first question of the scope definition process is as follows:

- *Q #1: What beneficial changes need to be implemented, and what is the associated project result as a whole?*

The other four questions (Q#2 to Q #5) are used in the course of the scope definition process as formulated in the previous section.

Taking into account the previous example (i.e., shortening the route of movement of raw materials in a workshop), *the implemented beneficial changes* (Q #1) create shorter unproductive time slots in the production process. *The associated project result* (also Q #1) implies:

- New layout of the production machinery; and
- New route of raw material movement.

The capabilities of the desired project result (Q #2), considering only the main capabilities, by means of which the above beneficial changes can be achieved, are:

- Safe movement of raw materials;
- Providing efficient supply for the production process.

Figure 4.2 conceptualizes the outcome of addressing Q #1 and Q 2.

Of course, a more detailed breakdown structure may also be required in the case of this project result as well.

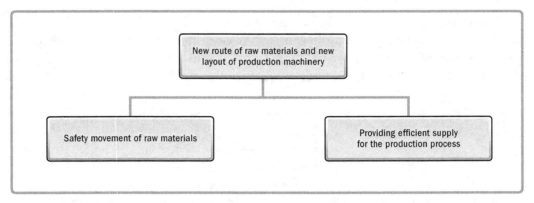

Figure 4.2 The main capabilities of a problem solving project result

Event Projects

There are organizations which regularly organize events that are considered to be projects. Good cases in point are the member organizations of a professional association. They need to organize conferences for their member professionals in a rotating manner. Indeed, it resembles a project since it has a predefined result to be achieved to budget and time. Moreover, the time is fixed, while this project also requires a temporary organization; however, the need for the project does not come from the organizational strategy shaped by the changing operational environment. Since it does not come from the strategy, the phenomenon of beneficial change could not be considered. The organization does not want to implement change; instead it wants to organize an event, and the event itself is the project result that should realize some goals. Thus, in the course of defining the expected project result, the owner organization of the event can also rely on the approach and method outlined in the previous section. Therefore, the first and the second questions should be modified as follows:

- *Q #1: What is the project result as a whole to be achieved?*
- *Q #2: What are the goals that should be realized by means of the project result?*

While the third (Q #3) and the fourth (Q #4) questions do not need change, the fifth one (Q #5) requires modification. Since in the second question instead of using the term capability is replaced by the term *goal*, it is wise to modify the fifth question (Q #5) as follows:

- *What are those means or goal providers (technical solutions, organizational solutions, processes etc.) that, being integrated as one particular project result, can realize the identified goals according to the specified quality and capability (or size or dimension) within the actual operational environment?*

Since the goals that are to be realized by means of the event as a project result are in the focus of scope definition in such a case, the associated structure is referred to as *goal breakdown structure*. Figure 4.3 illustrates a potential goal breakdown structure of a project that aims at organizing a world congress.

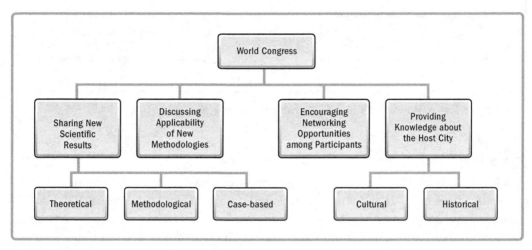

Figure 4.3 The goal breakdown structure of a world congress

Chapter 5

Viability of the Project Idea

The previous chapter introduced a strategy-oriented approach and methods to define the scope of the desired project result in compliance with a given (underlying) strategic objective. Therefore, by means of the capability breakdown structure, one can identify those capabilities that need to be provided by the desired project result. In other words, the question of for what the organization needs to use the desired project result is addressed. In order to achieve this end, not only should the required capabilities be identified, but the associated quality and capacity (or size or dimension) requirements need to be defined. At the same time, the decisive characteristics of the operational environment of the desired project result also need to be identified. Therefore the capability providers (either tangible or intangible) that can provide the identified capabilities according to the specified quality and capability (or size or dimension) requirements, within the revealed operational environment of the desired project result may be identified.

This latter issue is part of analyzing the viability of the project idea elaborated earlier. The viability analysis necessarily implies a multidimensional approach that may be ensured by elaborating far-sighted feasibility studies. The extant literature on feasibility studies is rather limited and vague. Most of the authors do not go further than emphasizing their importance; however, a few of them also emphasize the need for a multidimensional analysis.

This chapter aims at highlighting the role of feasibility studies in evaluating the viability of the elaborated project idea, and in making decisions on the desired project result. First, the aim of the feasibility studies and the associated requirements that need to be satisfied by these studies will be highlighted. This is followed by introducing the suggested multidimensional approach to elaborating feasibility studies. In this respect, the specific aim of each single study will be outlined. Finally, this chapter introduces the interrelationships between the strategy-oriented scope definition of the desired project result (including the role of feasibility studies) and the likely project success.

Requirements that Need to be Satisfied

The requirements that need to be met in the course of analyzing the viability of our project idea by means of the feasibility studies should be in compliance with the aim of the analysis. In order to consider the aim of feasibility studies properly, we need to consider the role of projects in the organization and the associated success criteria (see Chapter 1 and Chapter 2). From this point of view, we may state that the aim of the feasibility studies is to evaluate the viability of our project idea, formulated in terms of capabilities and both the associated quality and capacity requirements, under the likely conditions of its operational environment. Thus, the role of feasibility studies is not only to provide a basis for decision-making on the achievable project result, but to underpin the potential for the achievable success on the project as well. The aim and role of feasibility studies (i.e., of the viability analysis) justifies the need for a multidimensional approach to the analysis itself.

As to the viability analysis, the present literature (e.g., Stewart 2008) emphasizes the salient importance of the technical viability and financial viability (the business case-based viability). Notwithstanding, both the aspects of viability are important; however, these two aspects in themselves are not sufficient to underpin the potential for satisfying the implications of the complex phenomenon of project success. Earlier literature, however, placed greater emphasis on the non-quantitative side of project viability.

One of the most comprehensive publications on project feasibility was written by Clifton and Fyffe (1977). The authors, in the context of capital investment projects, suggest that the following aspects of the feasibility analysis should be considered:

- Market analysis
- Technical analysis
- Financial analysis
- Social profitability analysis

Lopes and Flawell (1998) also argue for the involvement of the non-quantitative aspects in the viability analysis of projects. The authors adopt a risk-centered perspective, and they suggest the involvement of all those aspects that might imply risk in the course of implementing the project. Therefore, they suggest considering the following viability/feasibility aspects and the associated analysis, in addition to the technical and financial aspects:

- The managerial role
- Strategic and synergistic effects with the rest of the organization
- Social analysis
- Political analysis
- Environmental analysis
- Organizational issues

The desired project results, at the same time, are considered to be complex systems, i.e. a defined complexity of interrelated parts (c.f. Miller 1971). While it is also true that there may be several versions of the desired project result to achieve a certain underlying strategic objective, the likely versions of a desired project result may occur:

- In terms of capabilities and the associated quality and capacity requirements; and
- In terms of the capability providers.

Therefore, we need to identify the most viable of these versions, and this need requires a comparison. Since the desired project results are also complex systems, in the course of this comparative evaluation, the following requirements should be met:

- Completeness of the evaluation criteria (i.e., all the relevant aspects of the viability need to be considered)
- Measurement of the evaluation criteria (i.e., for the sake of comparability, the value of each viability aspect needs to be translated into an ordinal variable)
- Dilemma of disqualification (i.e., the unacceptable value of a certain viability aspect may disqualify the entire project result, or one of its versions)
- Identifying the optimal combination of the available advantages and the acceptable disadvantages (i.e., selecting the best overall version of the project result)

The issue of measurement, and also both disqualification and optimal combination, are interrelated decision-making problems. There are a few good published methodologies by means of which one can solve these problems; thus, we turn our attention to the phenomenon of completeness of the analysis.

The Feasibility Studies

Bearing in mind the role of projects in organizations, and especially the associated success criteria, the author's research into a strategy-oriented approach to project management identified the following aspects of the viability analysis. which are commonly referred to as feasibility studies:

- Technical feasibility analysis
- Environmental feasibility analysis
- Stakeholder feasibility analysis
- Market feasibility analysis
- Financial feasibility analysis
- Implementation risk-related feasibility analysis
- Sustainability-related feasibility analysis
- Geographical location-related feasibility analysis

The list of the feasibility studies given above provides neither an order of importance nor a sequence of feasibility studies. However, the outcomes of the technical feasibility analysis may serve as the input for the other studies. At the same time, the outcomes of the other feasibility studies may affect the final outcomes of the technical feasibility analysis. The outcomes of any of the feasibility studies may have an impact on the capability breakdown structure and/or on the associated quality and capacity requirements elaborated and specified earlier. Consequently, the process of evaluating the viability of our project idea could also imply multiple iterations. The rest of this section focuses on the main objective that needs to be addressed in the course of elaborating different feasibility studies.

The technical feasibility study needs to reveal the desired project result in its tangible and/or intangible terms. The inputs for this study are the capability breakdown structure and both the associated quality and capacity requirements, and the emergent characteristics of the operational environment of the desired project result. Therefore, the technical feasibility study should reveal all those capability providers (both tangible and intangible) by means of which the identified capabilities can be realized under the condition of the likely operational environment in accordance with both the quality and capacity requirement. The outcomes of the technical feasibility study may be conceptualized—similarly to the product/assembly breakdown structure (see Bonnal et al. 2002)—in a *Capability Provider Breakdown Structure*. Figure 5.1 illustrates this structure, based on Figure 4.3 (organizing a world congress).

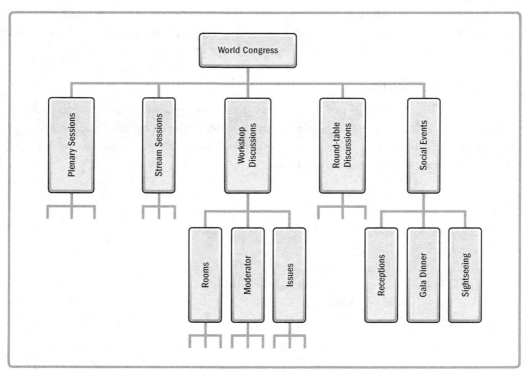

Figure 5.1 The capability provider breakdown structure of a world congress

There is a need for a technical feasibility study for any type of project. When there are several versions of the desired project result, each version may require a certain capability provider breakdown structure. However, the potential alternatives of the capability providers (as pointed out earlier) also may result in different versions of the capability provider breakdown structure.

The environmental feasibility study should address the question of whether the impact of the project on the environment is in compliance with the associated legislation. This issue needs to be considered regarding both the implementation process of the project and the operational life cycle of the project result. The environmental feasibility study is needed only when the project has a direct or indirect impact on the environment.

The stakeholder feasibility study aims to identify those who might have some vested interest either in the implementation process of the project or in the operational life cycle of the project result. This kind of feasibility study should also reveal the interest itself as influenced by the stakeholders, as well as the attitude of the stakeholders toward the project. Since there is no project without stakeholders, the stakeholder feasibility study is needed for all projects.

The market feasibility study analyzes market demand in terms of quantity, quality, and selling price. The outcomes may have a considerable impact on the project idea (e.g. capacity requirement) itself, while they may also have a considerable impact on the capability providers (e.g., the quality of them). The market feasibility study is needed only when the desired project result produces products or provides services to sell on the market.

The financial feasibility study implies a multi-fold aim:

- The likely implementation cost of the project and the associated cash-flow
- The potential financial resources and the associated cost of capital
- The financial benefits (e.g., net profit, cost saving, etc.) from the operational life cycle of the desired project result
- The likely financial return of the project implementation cost and the associated risk exposure

Since every project requires money to be implemented, and every project result is expected to generate financial benefits (directly or indirectly), a financial feasibility study is needed for any project.

The implementation risk-related feasibility study focuses on highlighting those risk factors and their sources that may have an impact on the implementation process, especially those impacting the likely duration time and the likely implementation cost. The implementation risk related feasibility study should be developed for all projects because of the uncertainty that is one of the inherent characteristics of any project.

The sustainability-related feasibility study basically implies a twofold aim, technical sustainability and financial sustainability. Technical sustainability focuses on the maintenance related issues of the completed project result, while financial sustainability focuses on the potential financial sources of maintenance. However, in the broader sense, sustainability may imply analyzing the potential for sustaining the beneficial change to be achieved by means of the desired project result. Thus, the sustainability-related feasibility study may be needed for any project.

The geographical location-related feasibility study considers the features of the potential geographical locations of the desired project result. So this type of feasibility study is needed for those projects that aim at creating a certain facility (e.g., building, road, factory, etc.).

When there is only one version of the project result, the professionals and decision-makers may identify whether it is viable based on the outcomes of the feasibility studies. At the same time, they may identify the changes by means of which the project idea might become viable. When there are several versions of the project result, each version should be considered in the feasibility studies. In such a case, the professionals and decision-makers need to identify the most viable version from amongst the viable ones. However, there are several published methodologies by means of which one can compare the different versions of the project idea. The following tabular arrangement and the associated scoring point system (a five- or ten-point scale) may help to summarize the outcomes of the feasibility analyses (see Figure 5.2).

Aspects of Viability \ Versions of the Project idea	Scoring Points Given to			
	A	B	C	D
Technical feasibility				
Environmental feasibility				
Stakeholder feasibility				
Market feasibility				
Financial feasibility				
Implementation risk-related feasibility				
Sustainability-related feasibility				
Geographical location-related feasibility				
Total Scores				

Figure 5.2 Framework for comparing the versions of a project idea

This section introduced the complexity of the viability analysis in terms of the feasibility aspects. In order to further explore this issue, we need to highlight the gains for project owners of using a strategy-based approach to scope definition.

Relationships Between Scope Definition and Success

The approach to scope definition of the desired project result introduced in the previous chapter is based on the need for achieving alignment between the scope of the desired project result and its underlying strategic objective. In order to satisfy this need, the author formulated five questions that need to be addressed in the course of translating a certain given strategic objective into a project result to be achieved. Based on the outcomes of addressing these questions appropriately, according to the research results of the author (Görög 2000), a project owner organization will have the potential for:

- A scope for the desired project result at the outset of the project that is in compliance with its underlying given strategic objective in terms of the required capabilities and the associated capacity (or size or dimension) and quality requirements. As to the achievable accuracy of scope definition in terms of details, it depends on the complexity of the underlying strategic objective and the inherent interdependence and the level of uncertainty regarding the strategic objective.
- Ensuring this compliance either in the case of changes to the underlying strategic objective or the changes to the project result (e.g., because of stakeholders) or when refining the project result (e.g., because of uncertainty).
- Marking off interrelated projects and making clear project boundaries which result in the potential for clarifying the responsibilities for the projects.
- Providing a focal point for evaluating the viability of the requested capabilities in accordance with the likely characteristics of the operational environment of the project result. The outcome of the technical feasibility study has a significant role since it results in the potential physical (tangible and intangible) structure of the project result.
- Reliable scope control in the course of implementing the project, since based on the physical structure of the project result, the structure of the capability providers (a product breakdown structure) can be developed. This structure is considered to be the basis of the baseline values for the scope control.
- Reliable process control in the course of implementing the project, since based on the structure of the capability providers (product breakdown structure), a reliable work breakdown structure may be developed. This work breakdown structure enables both resource allocation and scheduling, and activity-based cost estimation as well. Both time schedule and activity-based cost estimation are considered to be baseline values in the process control.

Taking into consideration the above-mentioned advantageous implications, one could say that the approach to scope definition introduced in the earlier chapter and the previously highlighted feasibility studies may contribute to achieving success on projects in many respects. The author's research outcomes justify this presumption. However, the contribution of the introduced approach to scope definition to achieving success on projects seems to be self-evident. The approach itself takes a certain strategic objective as the starting point of the scope definition, which results in the project idea in terms of capabilities and both the associated quality and capacity requirements.

At the same time, the feasibility studies are elaborated to evaluate the viability of the project idea. In this way, the feasibility studies also contribute to achieving success on the project. Table 5.1 conceptualizes how the different feasibility studies may determine the potential for achieving success on projects.

As Table 5.1 shows, all the success criteria identified in Chapter 2 are addressed directly or indirectly. Thus, the viability aspects involved in the feasibility studies meet the requirement of completeness of the evaluation criteria. That is, all the relevant and decisive aspects of the viability are considered. The complexity of the feasibility studies satisfy not only the requirements of the success criteria but that of the idea of justice as well (c.f. Sen 2009). This latter implies the need for considering each important aspect of a decision-making problem.

Chapter 4 pointed out the potential for multiple variations in the course of scope definition, while the chapter also drew attention to the need for flexibility and for the

Table 5.1 Relationships between feasibility studies and success criteria

Feasibility Studies	Contribution to Achieving Success in Terms of:	
	Directly	Indirectly
Technical feasibility	Client satisfaction	Project triangle Stakeholder satisfaction
Environmental feasibility	Stakeholder satisfaction	Client satisfaction Project triangle
Stakeholder feasibility	Stakeholder satisfaction	Client satisfaction Project triangle
Market feasibility	Client satisfaction	Stakeholder satisfaction Project triangle
Financial feasibility	Client satisfaction	Stakeholder satisfaction Project triangle
Implementation risk-related feasibility	Project triangle	Client satisfaction Stakeholder satisfaction
Sustainability-related feasibility	Client satisfaction	Stakeholder satisfaction
Geographical location-related feasibility study	Client satisfaction	Stakeholder satisfaction

potential danger of a premature scope freeze. Indeed, project scope definition is not an off-the-peg task; in many cases, it also needs to be undertaken in the course of implementing the project. The need for multiple variations was highlighted in connection with the feasibility studies as well. In brief again, multiple variations may occur since the outcomes of any feasibility study may have an impact not only on the other feasibility studies but on the capabilities and the associated quality and quality requirements as well.

In the rest of this section, the dilemma of flexibility versus scope freeze will be considered. Professionals often face this dilemma, since both flexibility and scope freeze are important. Scope freeze is needed for planning project implementation in a precise manner (efficiency), while flexibility is also needed because of uncertainty (Cleden 2009) and the associated potential for changes (effectiveness). Uncertainty may occur in many different forms, although a vague strategic objective may have a considerable impact not only on formulating the project idea but on analyzing the viability as well. However, the dynamics characteristic of the development of the potential capability providers is also of great importance from this point of view.

The higher the level of detail of both the capability breakdown structure and the capability provider structure, and the earlier the scope freeze is made, the higher the potential for planning the implementation of the project precisely. While the earlier the scope freeze is made, the higher the potential is for both a time- and a cost-consuming change process. These are the contradictions implied in the dilemma of flexibility versus scope freeze.

A strategy-oriented approach to project scope definition may make it easier to manage the dilemma of flexibility versus scope freeze to a certain extent by means of both the capability breakdown structure and the capability provider structure. Thus, the scope of the project result, and of course the viability analysis, may be considered at different levels for different capabilities and the associated capability providers. Those capabilities and the associated capability providers where uncertainty is low may be defined in detail, whereas these parts of the scope may be frozen. At the same time, those capabilities and the associated capability providers where uncertainty is high should not be defined in detail. These parts of the scope need flexibility, and need to be defined in detail probably in a milestone-event-by-milestone-event manner in the course of the implementation process.

Therefore, the scope of the desired project result is manageable in a modular manner, providing a compromise for the dilemma of flexibility versus too-early scope freeze. The above-highlighted compromise, however, may also be interpreted at the entire project level. In this way, it provides a solution for the so-called soft project (e.g., organizational development project) dilemma (see, e.g., Neal 1995; Atkinson,

Crawford, and Ward 2006) and for those projects which are based on emergent strategy. To define the scope in a modular manner appropriately necessitates considering the following potential relationships:

- Those parts of the scope that already have been both frozen and completed may have an impact on the parts under definition (in terms of capabilities and the associated quality and capacity requirement; moreover, also in terms of the capability providers)
- Defining a certain part of the scope in detail may necessitate reconsidering the characteristics of the likely operational environment of the project result
- Defining a certain part of the scope in detail may necessitate rework regarding previously completed parts

Chapter 6

Strategy-Oriented Scope Control and Change Management

Project control is an information system which supports making decisions in the course of implementing projects. The ultimate purpose of applying project control is to achieve success on the project. Project control should encompass both process control and scope control. Process control focuses on timely completion and the cost status of project implementation. Thus, process control may contribute to achieving success in terms of the project triangle.

At the same time, scope control focuses on the desired project result in terms of whether the actual status of the project result is in line with the desired project result outlined in the course of the scope definition. Consequently, scope control may contribute directly to achieving success in terms of client satisfaction. However, due to the interrelationships between the success criteria (see Chapter 2), both process control and scope control may contribute to achieving success in terms of stakeholder satisfaction as well.

Project control (i.e., process and scope control) is an information system since it provides information on the actual status of the project. The outcomes of comparing the actual status with the planned status of the project are the bases for making decisions on initiating and implementing corrective actions regarding the implementation process and the desired project result. Besides the corrective actions, there could be a need for changes regarding the desired project result initiated by the project owner in the course of implementation. These changes may have an impact on the implementation plans, while the status of the implementation itself may be the reason for initiating changes regarding the project result. However, the two types of control are interrelated. Both scope control and scope change are interrelated with the phenomenon of benefits management; moreover, benefits management may be considered to be part of scope management in general.

This chapter first addresses scope control of the desired project result and is followed by managing the change initiated by the owner organization regarding the project result. Finally, the interrelationships between scope definition, scope control, and scope change will be discussed from the point of view of achieving success on projects.

Controlling the Project Scope

Project control (i.e., process control and scope control) focuses on deviations from the actual status of plans, and these deviations can be positive or negative. Controlling the project implies a process which encompasses the following steps:

- Establishing baseline values
- Observing performance
- Analysis
- Correction

Project control as a process may be conceptualized in Figure 6.1 which shows clearly that the baseline values themselves may also undergo changes, generally due to the changes regarding the desired project result initiated by the project owner in the course of implementing the project.

Project control, even scope control, as an information system should satisfy the following needs in order to provide a basis for making decisions on initiating corrections:

- It must report deviations on a timely basis so that corrective actions could be initiated before more serious deviations actually occur. It may be ensured by means of the appropriate baseline values and the appropriate frequency of observing performance. (This issue will be further discussed in this section.)
- Its flow of information must relate to the project organizational arrangement (especially those who are involved in making decisions), while it must be sufficiently flexible because of the potential for the changing organizational context.

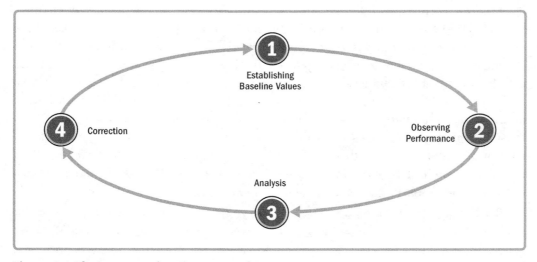

Figure 6.1 The process of project control

- It must be understood by those who use and operate it, otherwise the flow of information would be distorted. Thus, project control should not be used solely to call somebody to account in the case of unfavorable deviations.
- It should reduce to a language (e.g., exhibits, graphs, models) that permit a visual display that is easy to understand and comprehensive in its communication.

The first step of the control process (establishing baseline values) and the first need which should be satisfied (reporting deviations on a timely basis) are self-evidently of key importance in an appropriate scope control. Therefore, the rest of this section focuses on these two issues based on the implications of a strategy-oriented approach to scope definition of the desired project result.

It was pointed out earlier in this chapter that the ultimate purpose of controlling projects is to foster achieving success on the projects. It was also pointed out that scope control itself may contribute to achieving success in the first place in terms of client satisfaction. At the same time, the role of a project in an organization is to realize the implied beneficial change of the given underlying strategic objective. A strategy-oriented approach to scope definition of the desired project result takes this role of projects as a starting point for the scope definition itself. However, a strategy-oriented approach to scope definition of the desired project result provides only the potential for success. In order to actually achieve success on projects in terms of client satisfaction, the scope control should take its starting point from the strategically defined scope of the desired project result. That is, the approach to the scope control should also be strategy-oriented.

The baseline values are the norms against which the actual achievements (performance) need to be evaluated (analysis). The baseline values for the scope control, because of the required strategy-oriented approach, should be set up in the course of the scope definition, especially based on the breakdown structure of the final capability providers. However, the scope control needs to encompass not only the capability providers themselves but the associated documentation as well. These two types of baseline values are commonly referred to as deliverables (Bonnal, De Jonghe, and Ferguson 2006).

In order to define the baseline values, those parts of the desired project result need to be identified (based on the capability breakdown structure) that are describable in themselves by means of different parameters as the units of the project result. At the same time, baseline values are also those documents that describe these units of the project result, while these documents also need to be described by means of parameters. Therefore, the baseline values in the scope control may be direct or indirect constituents of the desired project result. The events during which these constituents (the deliverables) of the entire project result come into being in the course of project implementation are referred to as milestone events.

Taking into account the market penetration project considered in Chapter 4, a few of the likely baseline values may be:

- Documentation which demonstrates the safety of the product for the local health authority in accordance with local legislation and with local best practice;
- Documentation which highlights the business potential for local small shops in accordance with local legislation and with local best practice; or
- Documentation which demonstrates the business potential for local supermarkets in accordance with local legislation and with international best practice.

The actual status of the predefined parts of the desired project result and the associated other deliverables is evaluated by means of predefined parameters at predefined milestone events in the implementation process. When deviations occur from a certain predefined deliverable, it could lead to initiating and implementing corrections. These corrections regarding the achievable deliverable could imply reallocating resources and rescheduling the implementation process of the entire project. Therefore, the outcomes of the scope control should meet the outcomes of the process control since the potential for reallocating resources and rescheduling the implementation process depends on the actual status of implementation to a great extent.

Reporting deviations on a timely basis, besides the appropriately defined baseline values, is also of key importance to detect deviations when they may be corrected with relative ease. However, these two issues are strongly interrelated. The appropriate frequency of observing performance is determined by the likely number of potential baseline values (parts or units of the project result). At the same time, the likely number of these parts (units) of the desired project result is determined by:

- The level of detail of the desired project result by means of the capability provider breakdown structure, which, however, depends on the level of details applied in the capability breakdown structure; and
- The potential for ramifications regarding the scope of the project result (either in terms of capabilities or in terms of capability providers) that may occur in the course of implementing the project.

The lower the level of detail of the desired project result and the higher the potential for ramifications regarding the scope of the project result, the lower the number of parts (units) of the project result that may be predefined as baseline values for the scope control. The opposite relationship is also true. Figure 6.2 encapsulates these relationships.

Generally speaking, the higher the number of likely baseline values, the higher the potential for applying efficient scope control. Thus, the potential for the early

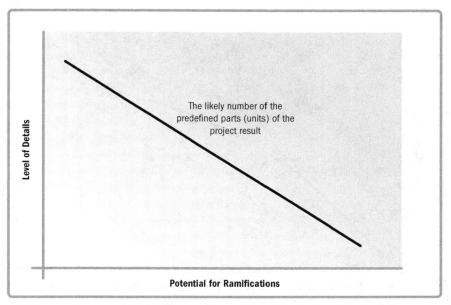

Figure 6.2 Determinants of the likely number of baseline values in the scope control

detection of the deviations may be increased. However, the cost efficiency of the scope control may not necessitate the use of all the likely baseline values. Cost efficiency in this respect implies the need for such a number of units and other deliverables (baseline values) by means of which the scope control may be undertaken in an efficient manner, that is, at the most economic cost. At the same time, the potential number of input-output relationships amongst the deliverables may also have a decisive impact on the appropriate number of baseline values. Figure 6.3 encapsulates these relationships.

The appropriate number of baseline values and the associated frequency of scope control need to be established on a project-by-project manner because of the uniqueness of each project result and the associated project context. However, the appropriate number of baseline values may be different (higher or lower) than the likely number of the baseline values. When at project level, the likely number of baseline values is lower than the appropriate number, the modular approach highlighted regarding the scope definition (see Chapter 5) is also applicable regarding the scope control.

Taking into consideration the above relationships, the following conclusions may be drawn:

- When the underlying strategic objective of a project is clearly defined (deliberate strategy) and/or the associated project result is quantitative in nature (hard project), there is a high potential for predicting the scope of the project result in detail. At the same time, there is no potential for ramifications in

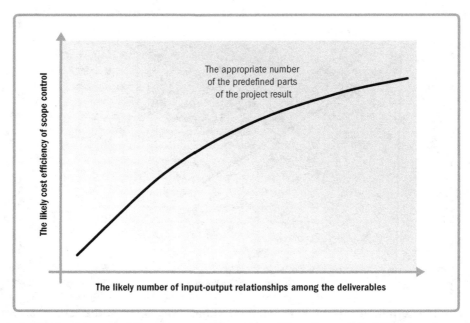

Figure 6.3 Determinants of the appropriate number of baseline values in the scope control

developing the project result. In such a case, there is a high potential for predefining the appropriate number of baseline values and for controlling the scope of the project result both efficiently and effectively.

- When the underlying strategic objective of a project is not clearly defined (emergent strategy) and/or the associated project result is qualitative in nature (soft project), there is no potential for defining the scope of the project result in detail. At the same time, there is a high potential for ramifications in developing the project result. In such a case there is a need for developing the desired project result in a modular manner. There is also a need for predefining the appropriate number of baseline values in a modular manner in order to control the scope of the project result both efficiently and effectively.

Managing the Scope Change

Contrary to scope control which aims at avoiding or minimizing deviations from the actually elaborated status, scope change is concerned with initiating changes regarding the previously elaborated status of the project result. The potential for managing scope changes smoothly is determined by the level of flexibility (Olsson 2006). While initiating changes may increase the effectiveness of the desired project result, they may decrease the efficiency of implementing the project. However, the likely impact of the changes (both in terms of time and cost) is generally lower in the early phases of the project. That is why flexibility (e.g., the modular approach to scope definition) may moderate the negative impact of scope changes.

A project owner organization needs to cope with managing changes throughout the life of the project in certain cases. Changes regarding the desired project result in the course of implementing the project may occur for a variety of reasons, namely:

- Ambiguous scope definition of the desired project result
- Change in the underlying strategic objective of the project
- Change in the likely operational environment of the desired project result
- Emerging new needs in the course of implementing the project due to rapid technical development
- Technical difficulties emerging in the course of implementing the project
- Changing stakeholder attitude, etc.

Atkinson et al. (2006) state that the common way of initiating change in the course of implementing the project is the deployment of change control procedures. They also highlight that design change will lead to change in schedule, cost, and the underlying resource allocation. Thus, scope change is related not only to scope control but process control as well. The literature on change management (e.g., Steffens, Martinsuo, and Artto 2007) focuses on the change process and the associated decision-making process. Söderholm (2008) emphasizes the importance of the state-gate decision points and the associated state-gate reviews in the change process. These tools may also be considered in the course of the scope control, especially when the underlying scope definition is developed in a modular manner. Instead of the change process, this section of the chapter, however, focuses on the approach to scope change itself.

Implementing changes regarding the desired project result requires a far-sighted, that is, strategy-oriented approach to managing the issue. Any change, whatever its reason is, involves the potential for deviation from the implied beneficial change of the actual underlying strategic objective of the project. However, a change initiated by the project owner organization needs to be in compliance with the actual state of the underlying strategic objective. The previously introduced strategy-oriented approach to scope definition (see Chapter 4 and Chapter5) also provides the potential for sustaining the compliance of the changed scope of the desired project result with the actual state of the underlying changing strategic objective.

A strategy-oriented approach to the scope definition problem postulates five questions that need to be addressed. Strategy-oriented change management also postulates questions that need to be addressed when changes are initiated in the course of implementing the project. These questions are as follows:

- *CQ #1 Are there new aspects of the implied beneficial changes according to the actual state of the underlying strategic objective?*
- *CQ #2 What is the likely impact of the initiated change on the predefined capabilities and the associated quality and capacity (or size or dimension) requirements?*

- *CQ #3 Are there new features of the likely operational environment of the changed project result that need to be considered?*
- *CQ #4 What is the impact of both the changed capabilities and the associated changed quality and capacity (or size or dimension) requirements, and the newly considered operational environment on the predefined capability providers?*

Depending on the reason for which the change is initiated, it may not be necessary to address all the questions. However, when the change of the underlying strategic objective is the reason, all the above questions should be addressed in order to sustain the compliance of the desired (changed) project result with the underlying changed strategic objective.

Interrelationships Between Scope Definition, Scope Control, Scope Change and Success

Projects are initiated in an organization to bring about a project result where the organization may realize the beneficial change inherent in the underlying strategic objective. That is why the approach to the scope definition of the desired project result needs to be strategy-oriented and why both scope control and change management regarding the scope of the desired project result also need to be strategy-oriented. At the same time, benefits management (e.g., Bennington and Baccarini 2004), especially in an IT/IS context, seems to be an emerging issue in project management. Therefore, benefits management, in general, encompasses realizing the potential benefits of a project result. In this way, benefits management should be related to the scope management in general.

Based on both an extensive literature review and their own research into benefits management, the above-cited authors stress the key role of benefits management. They state that benefits management is one of those factors which differentiates successful companies from less successful ones. At the same time, they state that project benefits do not happen by chance, thus, there is a need for formal benefits management from the outset of the project throughout its life cycle. At the same time, they found that project managers tend to manage the project deliverables instead of managing the benefits that may be achieved by means of the deliverables.

The last assertion of the authors is also acceptable, although the question as to what is the reason for the phenomenon described by the cited authors needs to be explored. In this respect, the author of this book relies on his research into both scope definition and project success on the one hand and on experience gained from consultancy over the years, on the other. However, first we need to have an insight into the phenomenon of benefits management. Based on previous publications, Bennington and Baccarini (2004) identify the following common steps in benefits management:

- Benefits identification (i.e., revealing the potential benefits of a given project result)
- Benefits realization planning (i.e., developing a plan as to how to realize the potential benefits)

- Benefits monitoring (i.e., comparing the results of the project with the benefits realization plan, and assessing the impact of changes on delivering the planned benefits)
- Benefits realization (i.e., comparing the actually delivered benefits with the planned benefits both on project completion and during the operational phase of the project result)

The benefits realization plan, as highlighted by the above-cited authors, encompasses the following steps:

- Where in the organization the benefits need to occur
- Who in the organization will enjoy the benefits
- Who in the organization is responsible for delivering the benefits
- How the benefits are linked to the project result
- Stakeholders' actions to ensure delivering the benefits
- When the benefits are realized

Central to the above approach is how the benefits are linked to the project result. Taking into consideration the scope definition of the desired project result (Chapter 4 and Chapter 5) and both the scope control and scope change outlined in this chapter on the one hand, and the proposed steps encompassed by the benefits realization plan on the other hand, the following notes need to be made:

- Both approaches address the same ultimate question (i.e., how the benefits are linked to the project result)
- Both approaches have the same ultimate purpose (i.e., providing the potential for organizational success by means of success achieved on projects)

However, despite the similarities, the underlying philosophy of the two approaches is quite different. The approach implied in the benefits management perspective externalizes the issue of managing the realizable benefits. Thus, it is considered to be some "add-on" perspective to managing projects. At the same time, the approach of a strategy-oriented scope definition (including feasibility studies) and both the associated scope control and scope change internalize the phenomenon of benefits delivered by the project result for the owner organization. Therefore, benefit management is implied not only in the scope definition but both in scope control and scope change. That is why a strategy-oriented approach to managing the scope of the desired project result implies higher potential for achieving success on the entire project.

Due to the lack of a strategy-oriented approach either to the scope definition of the expected project result or to both scope control and scope change, project managers are inclined to manage the project deliverables instead of managing the benefits that may be achieved by means of the deliverables. Therefore, the project seems to be externally given for project managers. In other words, the lack of a strategy-oriented approach leads to managing only the deliverables of the project, which, at the same time, may lead at best to success only in terms of the project triangle.

Chapter 5 highlighted the advantages that may be gained by project owner organizations when they apply a strategy-oriented scope definition of the desired project result and prepare feasibility studies. Thus, one should say that a strategy-oriented scope definition underpins the potential for success achievable on projects in terms of:

- The project triangle
- Client (owner) satisfaction; and
- Stakeholder satisfaction.

However, by means of a strategy-oriented scope control and scope change, the potential for success in each the previously listed terms may be sustained. This is not to say that a strategy-oriented approach applied in these respects guarantees success; however, without this approach resulting success is a fortunate accident. The interrelationships highlighted above are encapsulated in Figure 6.4.

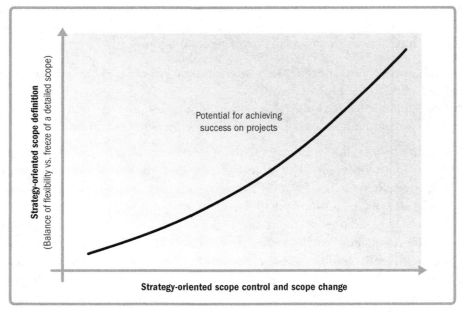

Figure 6.4 Interrelationships between scope definition, scope control, scope change, and success

Chapter 7

Project Post-Evaluation

Most of those authors who provide a comprehensive introduction to project management (e.g. Lock 1992; Cleland 1994; Gido and Clements 1999) also address the issue of project termination. However, only a few of them are concerned with the phenomenon of post-evaluation, and they adopt a very superficial-level approach to this issue. This means that generally only a few sentences are devoted to emphasizing the importance of project post-evaluation. At the same time, because of the underlying non-strategy-oriented (linear) project cycle, the authors mainly emphasize the phenomenon of learning from experience (e.g., Leybourne 2007).

Therefore, the author of this book does not rely on earlier related publications, as a strategy-oriented approach to project implementation necessitates a strategy-oriented post-evaluation of the completed project result as well. This chapter aims to highlight a framework by means of which one can develop a tailor-made post-evaluation procedure in detail for a given project. The proposed framework is derived from experience gained from consultancy over the years.

Based on a strategy-oriented approach to project implementation, this short chapter firstly introduces the primary aim of post-evaluation, which is followed by highlighting the steps involved in the post-evaluation cycle. Finally, the role of a project office in the evaluation process will be introduced briefly.

It is worth emphasizing at the beginning of the chapter that an objective project post-evaluation necessitates an independent team of evaluators in the project owner organization. This team, however, may involve the project manager as well.

The Aim of Post-Evaluation

Chapter 3 points out that the post-evaluation phase of a strategy-oriented project cycle has a twofold aim. One of them is the evaluation of success achieved on the project, while the other is the evaluation of the project management process. However, this latter issue is wisely imbedded in the organizational learning process. Since the role of projects in organizations is to achieve strategic objectives, the first aspect of post-evaluation, that is, the success achieved on project, will be further interpreted.

At the same time, Chapter 2 highlights the concept of the hierarchical approach to project success. Here, the success achieved on projects is measured against the project triangle, client satisfaction, and stakeholder satisfaction. Because of the role of the projects in organizations, client satisfaction (i.e., the extent to which a completed project result may contribute to achieving the underlying strategic objective), has a central role to a certain extent. Although the success criteria are interrelated, both serious deficiencies in the project triangle and the lack of stakeholder satisfaction may minimize the potential for achieving the underlying strategic objective.

Taking into account the above considerations, we may conclude that the primary aim of post-evaluation is to evaluate the extent to which a completed project result may contribute to achieving the underlying strategic objective. In the wider sense of the term, post-evaluation implies the likely effectiveness of a completed project result. This conclusion is not saying that the other two criteria are negligible. However, the potential for evaluating the success rate against these two criteria is quite different. The evaluation against the project triangle may be completed with ease in a quantitative manner, while the evaluation of stakeholder satisfaction may be a very difficult undertaking. The difficulty in this respect is rooted in two fundamental reasons, namely the implied subjectivity on the stakeholder side, and the associated potential for the changing stakeholder attitude toward the project and its likely outcomes.

Although the primary aim of post-evaluation is the assessment of how the completed project result may contribute to achieving the underlying strategic objective, the evaluation of managing the project may also belong to the post-evaluation in the wider sense of the term. Evaluating the project management process is, in other words, evaluating the success of managing the project, which may be undertaken in combination with the organizational learning process.

Taking into consideration the above-identified primary aim of the project post-evaluation, we may conclude that this need for feedback on the scope definition of the project result, whereas post-evaluation also becomes a strategy-oriented task. This feedback makes it possible to define the primary aim of the post-evaluation in a more specific way. Thus, the aim of post-evaluation is to reveal whether the completed project result is in compliance with the desired project result, that is, whether it may provide the actually predefined capabilities in accordance with:

- The actually defined quality requirements; and
- The actually defined capacity (or size or dimension) requirements in the actual context of the operational environment of the project result.

Thus, post-evaluation should overlap with the tests (trials) of the completed project result. The potential lack of the above-specified compliance will restrict the achievement of the underlying strategic objective, although it depends on the extent of the actual incompliance. In other words, revealing the potential deviations between the desired project result and the completed project result highlights, at the same time, the potential for achieving the underlying strategic objective, that is, the potential success rate in terms of client satisfaction.

The Process of Post-Evaluation

Bearing in mind the primary aim of post-evaluation and its inevitable overlap with the tests of the completed project result, the strategy-oriented post-evaluation process comprises the following steps:

- Tests of the completed project result;
- Revealing deviations;
- Evaluating the potential for client satisfaction; and
- Formulating alternatives for improvement.

These interrelated steps of the process may be conceptualized in Figure 7.1.

The tests of the completed project result aim to evaluate whether the completed project result can provide the predefined capabilities according to both the quality and capacity requirements in the actual operational environment. This complex aim postulates an also-complex process that encompasses the following steps:

- Precomissioning, that is, checking on the functional completeness of the completed project result, and the associated no-load tests. For example, whether all the predefined menu-bars are accomplished and can be opened, etc., in the case of an information system.

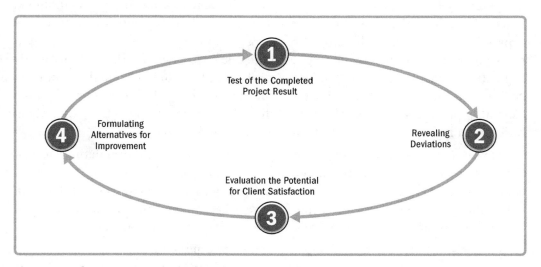

Figure 7.1 The strategy-oriented project post-evaluation cycle

- Start up, that is, a series of load tests up to the specified capacity both in normal and extreme conditions. For example, uploading data over the predefined capacity, uploading false data, and so forth, in the case of an information system.
- Trials, that is, measuring output parameters and/or efficiency (quality) during a predefined time period. For example, response time in the case of an information system.

Revealing deviations, as part of the post-evaluation process also overlaps with testing the completed project result. This step aims to highlight the deviations of the actually completed project result from the desired project result. Presuming that changes were initiated and implemented regarding the project result when the underlying strategic objective underwent changes, deviations may occur:

- In terms of both functional and non-functional capabilities;
- In terms of both quality and capability requirements; and
- Due to the different characteristics of the operational environment.

These deviations, however, may imply the incompatibility of the capability providers as well. Based on experiences accumulated from consultancy over the years, it might be stated that the potential for serious deviations is considerably higher in the case of soft projects (e.g., organizational development) than in the case of hard projects (e.g., real estate development). It is due to the lower potential for defining the scope of the desired result of the soft projects in detail, while the hard projects imply a higher potential for an accurate scope definition.

Evaluating the potential for client satisfaction might be undertaken based on the revealed deviations. Generally speaking, the smaller the deviations, the higher the potential for achieving client satisfaction. In fact, this potential is determined by the form in which the deviation occurred, and the implied flexibility of the capability providers (i.e., the project result itself) to a great extent. When the capability providers have the flexibility to tune the quality or increase the capacity easily (e.g., an information system), or accommodating them to the actual operational environment, the potential for client satisfaction may be higher. However, when the capability providers do not include flexibility (e.g., a bridge), the potential for client satisfaction may be lower, even in the case of a smaller deviation.

However, the issue of likely client satisfaction leads us to formulating suggestions for improvement when deviations occur. At the same time, due to the uniqueness of the project results and the project context, we need to bear in mind that both the evaluation of the likely potential for client satisfaction and the formulation of alternatives for improvement require an individual approach to each case.

Formulating alternatives for improvement is determined by:

- The feature of the deviations (capability, quality, etc.);
- The extent of the deviations;

- The extent of flexibility implied in the capability providers; and
- The entire project context (the underlying strategic objective, future potentials, the organizational culture etc.).

Formulating feasible (viable) alternatives for improvement requires literally an individual approach to each project.

The Role of the Project Office

Nowadays, especially in a multi-project environment, the role of the project office has an emerging importance. However, the terms project office and program office are sometimes used interchangeably, since in a multi-project environment the basic roles of the two kinds of office are basically the same. However, as there are a few different solutions experienced in the practice of the organizations, two typical solutions may be identified:

- The project office is the organizational unit which exercises line authority over the project managers.
- The project office is a staff-like unit which provides a liaison with the project director who exercises line authority over the project managers, while the staff provides professional assistance both to the project director and the project managers.

This latter solution is conceptualized in Figure 7.2 in the context of a project-oriented organizational arrangement.

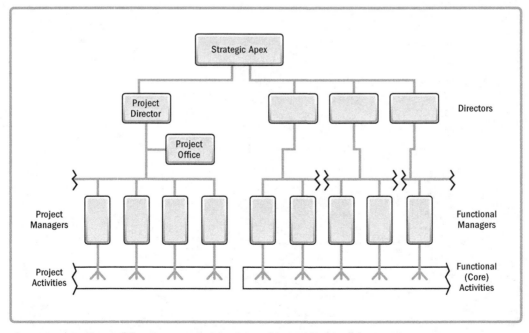

Figure 7.2 Project office in a project-oriented organizational arrangement

The author is not going to provide a comprehensive introduction to the project office; instead, the post-evaluation related role of this office will be highlighted. In doing so, the project office as a staff-like unit (see Figure 7.2) will be considered, since this arrangement implies the potential for an independent post-evaluation. Therefore, the project office may undertake the following post-evaluation related tasks:

- Develop and maintain organization-wide standard methodology for post-evaluation
- Develop tailor-made procedures for each completed project result based on the standard methodology
- Provide assistance for the evaluation team

As stressed earlier in this chapter, the post-evaluation of the completed project result should be undertaken by an independent evaluation team, although it is wise to involve the project manager and a professional from the project office.

Chapter 8

Implications for Program Management

Chapter 1 of this book points out that an organizational project portfolio may comprise both single projects and project programs. However, subsequent chapters address a strategy-oriented approach to project implementation with a focus on single projects. Thus, the previous chapters highlight, among others, a strategy-oriented scope definition of the desired project result and the associated feasibility studies, and the strategy-oriented scope control and scope change in the case of single projects.

This chapter is going to address these issues at a higher level, that is, at the level of project programs. Although there is considerable literature on program management, there is no agreement on how to translate single project management knowledge to program management (Thiry and Deguire 2007). Moreover, there is not one broadly accepted definition as to what project programs are.

Based on research (Görög 2011) into managing project programs undertaken by the author of this book, this chapter first provides an interpretation of the phenomenon of project programs. Then the strategy-oriented scope management introduced in the previous chapters at single project level will be interpreted at the level of project programs.

Project Programs

Although both the phenomena of project portfolio and project programs are not new amongst academics and practitioners, there are still many ambiguities in terms of definitions, and the two terms are often used interchangeably. Chapter 1 of this book briefly highlights the differences between the phenomena of project portfolio and project program. Program level strategy-oriented scope management, however, necessitates going into details as to what constitutes a project program. To achieve this end, it seems to be wise to overview the different views on this phenomenon.

Turner and Müller (2003) approach the issue from the perspective of single projects. They state that project programs are frameworks that provide strategic direction for a group of projects, while a project portfolio aims at providing efficient resource utilization across the projects that the program encompasses. Lycett, Rassau. and Danson (2004) provide a critical review of earlier approaches to programs and their management. They state that program management suffers from two flawed assumptions, namely:

- Program management is considered to be scaled-up project management; and
- There is a single form for managing programs.

In the view of Gareis (2004), a project program is a temporary organization but contrary to a single project (which is also a temporary organization, according to Gareis), a program implies a unique and long-term process of large scope. Morris and Jamieson (2005) provide a comprehensive picture of projects, project programs, and project portfolios based on the approach of the authors of previously published papers. These authors themselves do not provide new definitions, but they emphasize the extremely important role of projects, project programs, and project portfolios in forming and implementing organizational strategic objectives.

Blomquist and Müller (2006) stress that project portfolios are management decision frameworks, and they are used to identify those projects that need to be implemented in order to achieve strategic objectives. These authors also emphasize that project portfolio management is a governance method for selecting and prioritizing resource-interrelated projects in organizations. They point out that program management is different from portfolio management, though they are connected. Program management, in their view, focuses on defining the desired goals of the individual projects in a specific manner. Project management is then used to complete these projects in an efficient way.

Pellegrinelli et al. (2007) highlight the strategic role of project programs, and program management is considered by them to be the means that brings about planned changes (strategic objectives) in organizations. In their view, program management is first of all an inter-project coordination mechanism for achieving desired change. Martinsuo and Lehtonen (2007a; 2007b) do not differentiate clearly between project portfolio and project program (i.e., the phenomenon of a project program is considered to be identical to the phenomenon of project portfolio). These authors emphasize that project portfolio (or multi-project) management is concerned with a group of projects that are competing with each other for the same resources in order to maximize strategic benefit under the supervision of top management. According to Aubry et al. (2007), both portfolio and program management are considered to be organizational project management with the aim of achieving organizational strategic objectives.

Thiry (2004a; 2004b; 2007), similarly to Blomquist and Müller (2006), emphasizes that program management is not just scaled up project management; instead, it is the governance of a number of interrelated projects. Thiry also states that project portfolio management is a process that aims at both analyzing and allocating organizational resources to projects and project programs in order to achieve organizational objectives and create value for the stakeholders. Maylor et al. (2006), making reference to Andersen and Jessen (2003), highlight the definite distinction between the terms project management, project program management, and project portfolio management. Here, project management involves managing single projects, while project program management is concerned with a group of projects that have a common objective. Project portfolio management involves the management of a collection of projects and project programs that do not necessarily have a common objective but they are undertaken simultaneously.

Milosevic et al. (2007) emphasize that program management is the coordinated management of interdependent projects. The *PMBOK® Guide* (Project Management Institute 2008) also states clearly that a program is a group of related projects that are managed in a coordinated manner. However, none of these books reveal the way in which the projects in a program are interdependent or related to each other.

Although most of the authors quote basically the same concepts regarding both project portfolio management and project program management, there is some ambiguity as to what specifically differentiates a project program from a portfolio of projects. Project portfolio management is considered to be an organization-wide strategic issue that encompasses all those projects that need to be implemented in order to realize organizational strategic objectives. Therefore, a certain project portfolio is a means of achieving planned change in an organization. At the same time, project program management—similarly to project management—is concerned with implementing the project portfolio. The relationship between these two phenomena does not imply that the concept of project program is identical to the concept of project portfolio. We need to bear in mind that the projects of a program are interrelated in some way, while, the projects of an entire portfolio could encompass individual projects as well.

In order to understand what makes a project program, we need to clarify what defines the interrelationships between the projects of a program. If the common strategic objective is considered to be the only link that connects a group of projects as one program, we cannot differentiate the phenomenon of project portfolio from the phenomenon of project program, since at a higher level of the hierarchic structure of organizational strategy (see Figure 1.1), the aim of each project is to realize the same final strategic goals. In other words, in this way, a certain project portfolio of an organization would be a single project program.

Research into managing project programs, recently completed by the author (Görög 2011) identified the following two significant interrelationships—besides the common strategic objective—regarding the projects encompassed by a program:

- Resource-related interdependence (i.e., common resources are needed by the projects of a program to implement the program itself)
- Scope-related interdependence (i.e., a certain outcome of a project in the program depends on the actual outcomes of other projects in the program, and vice versa)

These interrelationships make it possible to differentiate project programs from single projects within a project portfolio. Thus, a project portfolio encompasses all those projects that need to be implemented in an organization in order to achieve the actual set of strategic objectives. Projects in a project portfolio implemented without considering the resource use of other projects and/or without considering the actual status of other project results which are being implemented are referred to as individual or single projects. On the other hand, those projects in a portfolio that are connected by means of a common resource pool (resource-related interdependence) and/or by means of scope-related interdependence are considered to be one program. As to resource-related interdependence, it should be noted that we do not consider time and money, the two special types of resources that otherwise should be taken into account in the case of project portfolio management. An organizational project portfolio may comprise both single projects and project programs, even though the two extremes—only single projects or only one single program—may also occur.

Therefore, in the next section of this chapter, the term project program is understood as a group of projects which are interrelated due to the common resource pool (resource-related interdependence) and/or by means of scope-related interdependence.

Strategy-Oriented Program-Level Scope Management

Based on a single project perspective, central to a strategy-oriented approach to project implementation, as pointed out in the earlier chapters, are:

- The strategy-oriented scope definition of the desired project result and the associated feasibility studies;
- The strategy-oriented scope control; and
- The strategy-oriented scope change.

The approach applied at single-project level will be translated now to the level of project programs. However, we need to bear in mind that a project program is more than a group of projects. The interrelationships characteristic of projects in a program—whether they are scope-related or resource-related—involve a new quality and complexity of programs.

Defining the Scope of the Desired Program Result

Defining the scope of the desired program result and the associated scope of the project results that belong to the program is one of the most difficult program management tasks. Similarly to the case of single projects, from a strategic point of view the scope definition is of great importance. The degree of accuracy of the scope definition will determine the degree of accuracy of preparing the implementation plans, especially the resource allocation, which may be uncertain due to the vague scope. Ultimately, the weak scope definition of the desired program result (and its projects' results) might impede achieving the underlying strategic objective of the program. The need for clear scope definition of the program result and its projects is a doubly justified need.

Thiry (2004a; 2004b) argues that the scope definition of a program result should be based on a less formal and cognitive process. However, the required cognitive nature depends on the clarity of the underlying strategic objective. If this strategy is vague (e.g. emergent strategy), while there is potential for alternatives, a less formal and more cognitive process of program scope definition is required. In such a case, strategy formulation and both portfolio and program definition may be done as one process (see Grundy and Brown 2002). Although, in the case of firm strategy (e.g., deliberate strategy), when the strategic objectives are derived from analysis and planning, while the associated project portfolio is identified, the program definition process may become a more formal process. Recently published books (e.g., Moore 2009; Morris and Pinto 2007; Rad and Levin 2006) provide practical insights into how to ensure the right organizational project portfolio.

Regardless of the nature of the process that brings about the strategic objectives, we need to define those projects and programs that should be implemented in order to achieve organizational strategic objectives. The approach and method introduced in Chapter 4 in a single-project context are also applicable in a program context in order to define the scope of the entire program result. To illustrate the applicability of the approach and method, let us consider the following case program of a transporting company. The underlying strategic objective of the program was increasing the market share of the company. In order to achieve this end, there was a need for developing the operational competences of the company. That is, according to the implied beneficial change, creating new competences so that the company would become a forwarding agent being able to organize forwarding goods by truck, by train, and by ship. The program encompasses the following projects:

- Business process development, and both the associated organizational structure and information system development
- Establishing strategic partnerships with transporting companies that have alternative transporting capacities
- Setting up a logistics center

Figure 8.1 illustrates the capability breakdown structure of the operational competency development program.

This figure is only an illustration, and it does not aim to reveal the scope in detail of the whole program result. It focuses on the main functional capabilities of the desired program result.

Identifying the required capabilities of the expected program result makes it possible to specify both quality and capacity (or size or dimension) requirements for each capability, though this task requires a more detailed structure elaboration. Based on the identified capabilities and the specified quality and capacity (or size

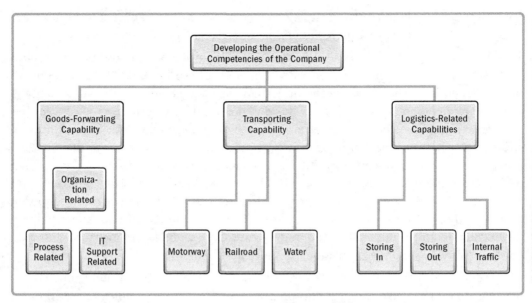

Figure 8.1 Capability breakdown structure of the operational competency development program

Source: Görög (2011, 28)

or dimension) requirements, and also based on the features that are characteristic of the operational environment of the program result, we can identify those means (capability providers) that physically create the desired program result.

Similarly to the case of single projects, the program-level capability breakdown structure also provides the starting point to evaluate the feasibility of the program. At the same time, this structure, and the associated breakdown structure of the capability providers (product breakdown structure), also make it possible to mark off the boundaries of the projects within the program and define responsibilities. Finally, these structures also make it possible to identify clearly the activities (by means of the WBS technique) that bring about both program and project results. A clear and reliable work breakdown structure will be the basis for preparing the implementation plans for the program and its projects. At the same time, the structure of the capability providers makes it possible to define those parts (units) of both the desired program result and the implied project results that are used as baseline values (norms) in the course of the scope control.

Scope Control and Scope Change

Similarly to the case of single projects, the bases of the *scope control* should be set up in the course of the program scope definition. It is of great importance in the case of those programs in which the projects are connected by means of scope-related interdependence. For each desired project result which is derived from the entire desired program result, those deliverables need to be identified that may be evaluated by means of predefined parameters at the milestone events in the implementation process. When deviations occur, it could lead to such corrections that might have an impact on other projects (results) and/or other associated deliverables of the program. These corrections regarding the desired result could imply reallocating resources and rescheduling the implementation process of the whole program. Therefore, the outcomes of the scope control should meet the outcomes of the process control, since the potential for reallocating resources and rescheduling the implementation process depends on the actual status of implementation to a great extent. It is especially important when the projects of a program are connected by means of resource-related interdependence as well. Therefore, we should stress again the need for a strategy-oriented approach to the scope control.

Initiating and implementing *scope change* in a program context is also a difficult program management task. The need for changes to the desired program result may occur basically for the same reasons that were mentioned in Chapter 6 in a single-project context. While it is also true that sustaining a certain degree of flexibility by means of the modular approach to scope definition may moderate the negative impact (lower efficiency of implementation) of scope changes. At the same time, the use of both the state-gate decision points and the associated state-gate reviews may be beneficial in a program context as well.

The approach to implementing changes in a program context needs to be definitely strategy-oriented and even more far-sighted than in a single project context. Any change implies not only the potential for deviation from the implied beneficial change of the actual underlying strategic objective but the potential for interrelated changes regarding the projects of the program as well. In other words, the scope change regarding one of the projects in the program may have an impact on the scope of the other project results also belonging to the program. It is especially characteristic of those programs in which the projects are connected by scope-related interdependence. A change initiated by the program owner organization needs to be in compliance not only with the actual state of the underlying strategic objective but the scope of the interrelated project results as well.

In Chapter 6, four questions (CQ #1 to CQ #4) were formulated that need to be addressed in order to manage the scope change in line with the actual state of the underlying (changing) strategic objective in a single-project context. However, now these questions should be interpreted in the context of a project program as follows:

- CQ #1 needs to be addressed at program level.
- CQ #2 needs to be addressed at program level in the first place, and the consequential changes need to be addressed also at the level of projects that belong to the program.

- CQ #3 needs to be addressed at program level in the first place, and the consequential changes need to be addressed also at the level of the projects that belong to the program.
- CQ #4 needs to be addressed at the level of projects that belong to the program.

Similar to the case of implementing change in a single-project context, when the change of the underlying strategic objective is the reason for initiating change regarding the desired program result, all the questions should be addressed in order to sustain the compliance of the desired (changed) program result (and that of its projects) with the underlying changed strategic objective.

Part II

A Strategy for Implementing External Projects—The Client Perspective

Chapter 9

Project Implementation Strategy

Nowadays, the phenomenon of project strategy is an emerging issue in the project management literature; however, there is no one broadly accepted interpretation of the term. Morris and Jamieson (2005) adopt a broad approach when the authors say that project strategy implies transforming business strategy into project objectives, and also both those predefined processes and practices that are used in the course of implementing the project. Artto et al. (2008), based on an extensive literature review, created a more specific definition of the project strategy: "Project strategy is a direction in a project that contributes to success of the project in its environment" (ibid., 8). The word *direction* implies goals, plans, tools, and methods, etc., as the explicit elements of the project strategy.

Project implementation strategy, in this way, may be understood as one of the elements of project strategy. However, the project implementation strategy is of great importance from the point of view of achieving success in external projects.

This chapter provides an interpretation of project implementation strategy in an external project context. In order to achieve this end, the phenomenon of external projects and its primary stakeholders will be introduced. First, however, different views on the topic are highlighted in brief.

Views on Contracting Out Projects

In the project management literature, different terms are used for contracting out projects. Both the terms procurement and purchasing are used interchangeably, however, the term supply-chain management also appears nowadays. Fleming (2003) emphasizes the importance of selecting the type of contract, which—in his terms—means selecting a certain type of payment. Schwalbe (2004) identifies six steps in the procurement process, beginning with a make-or-buy decision, and concluding with contract close-out.

Bower and Smith (in Smith 1995) emphasize the need for establishing a formalized contract policy which encompasses why, what, when, and how the projects will be contracted out.

Lawson (in Lawson et al. 1999) uses the term project execution strategy in a much wider sense than the procurement itself; however, her term also implies the procurement-related tasks. Lawson emphasizes that project execution strategy is at the heart of managing external projects since it determines the direction of future work. Bower (in Bower, 2003a) approaches this issue based on the supply-chain perspective. In her view, the phenomenon of contract strategy (contracting out work) is understood as part of project procurement. Bower also emphasizes that making decisions on contract strategy is one of the most important decisions of a client organization, which implies decision-making on payment as well. Ward (2008) addresses the problem within the wider context of purchasing, however, he follows the traditional approach to contracting out.

Turner (in Turner 2009) develops a systematic approach to selecting implementation strategy; however, he also uses the term contract strategy. He suggests a selection methodology that is primarily based on which of the primary stakeholders controls the risk (for further details, see Chapter 12).

The author of this book uses the term project implementation strategy to mean the contracting out of work during the project implementation phase. This term is used for three reasons:

- It is in line with the emerging phenomenon of project strategy.
- Making decisions on the method based on which the work in the implementation phase of a project is contracted out is a strategic issue. It determines the future of the project.
- The term project implementation strategy, as it will be used in this book, implies a broader scope in comparison with the traditional contract strategy. However, it is a more narrow term than both supply chain management and procurement management.

External Projects and the Primary Stakeholders in External Projects

Projects may be grouped into two basic categories based on those contributors who are implementing a project. One of them is referred to as internal projects, where the work in the project implementation process is implemented by the resources of the project owner organization. Another category of projects comprises those projects that utilize external resources during their implementation. Thus, the latter group of projects is considered to be external since the work encompassed by the implementation process is contracted out. In this way, the external projects may be referred to as outsourced projects. Although both terms are used nowadays, the author adopts the use of the term *external* in this book.

Primary stakeholders in an external project may be grouped into two categories, namely:

- The project client; and
- The external contributors

The project client is the organization that initiates a project in order to achieve a certain organizational objective. The client's role is of great importance in any project, since this is the primary stakeholder who needs to make all final decisions in connection with implementing the project. However, the client entrusts a project manager with managing the project, while the client organization may also rely on a sponsor and/or a supervisory board to ensure the proper implementation of the project. At the same time, the client may be assisted by different internal consultants as well.

The role of the potential external contributors may vary from project to project, depending on the type of project in question. Nevertheless, the most typical external contributors are the contractor, the supplier, the consultant, the designer, the surveyor, etc.

When considering the phenomenon of project implementation strategy, we need to consider only those stakeholders who are involved in the following tasks in the course of implementing the project:

- Implementing the work in the project; and
- Managing the implementation of the work.

In this way, when project implementation strategy is at the forefront, we need to consider:

- The client of the project, regardless of the person or the body who represent the client organization. Thus, throughout this book, this stakeholder is referred to as the client.
- Those external contributors who are directly involved in the implementation process (contractors, designers, etc.), that is, those external stakeholders who have a direct stake in implementing the work (who do the work). Throughout this book, these stakeholders are commonly referred to as external contributors.

These stakeholders may be referred to as the primary stakeholders in the project implementation process, since they play an active role in the project. Other external stakeholders, such as consultants, surveyors, suppliers, etc., are not considered, since they are not involved in implementing the work in a direct way. Consequently, they do not have a direct stake in the implementation process.

The Role of Project Implementation Strategy

The phenomenon of project implementation strategy is related to the project triangle, that is:

- The project result as a whole, including its completeness, its operability, and its quality;
- The entire duration time of implementing the whole project; and
- The total cost of implementing the whole project.

In the case of an internal project, the client is the only primary stakeholder who is involved in both implementing and managing the project work. Consequently, the client is the only organization that needs to take and bear all those responsibilities and risks that are associated with the project triangle. At the same time, in external projects, those responsibilities and risks that emerged in the implementation phase of the project need to be shared among those primary stakeholders who are involved in implementing and managing the project work in the implementation phase of the project.

Accordingly, project implementation strategy is understood in this book as a means of allocating those responsibilities and risks between the client and the external contributors which are associated with the project triangle in the course of the implementation phase of the project. The toolkit by means of which these responsibilities and risks may be allocated encompasses both types of contract and types of payment (Görög & Smith 1999). The types of contract and the types of payment have a different role in allocating the responsibilities and risks associated with the project triangle.

Types of contract are the means by which the responsibilities and the risks that are associated with the expected project result in its entirety and for the entire duration time of the implementation phase are allocated among the primary stakeholders. Thus, contract types are differentiated based on the extent to which a certain contractual arrangement shifts the majority of the above-mentioned responsibilities and risks onto the client or the external contributors.

Types of payment are the means by which the risks and responsibilities that are associated with the cost occurring in the client organization in the course of the implementation phase of the project are allocated between the primary stakeholders of the project implementation process. Thus, payment types are differentiated based on the extent to which a certain type of payment shifts the majority of the above-mentioned risks and responsibilities onto the client or the external contributors. Accordingly, types of payment are classified as price-based, cost-based, and target-based.

Since the types of contract and the types of payment have a different role in project implementation strategy, these two phenomena need to be clearly differentiated.

However, the early literature did not pay attention to this task. The following chapters (Chapters 10 to 12) provide a short introduction to how the approaches to project implementation strategy, and the types of contract and types of payment evolved over the last few decades. Notwithstanding these efforts, there is no one unanimously accepted concept amongst professionals. Differentiating the phenomena of types of contract and types of payment is justified by the fact that they are different by nature. In this way, the two kinds of tools can allocate different kinds of responsibilities and risks, as it was pointed out earlier in this chapter.

Differentiating the two kinds of tools provide the potential for combining them in the course of implementing external projects in order to formulate an appropriate project implementation strategy. An appropriate project implementation strategy implies the appropriate allocation of those responsibilities and risks that are associated with the project triangle. The project triangle—besides client satisfaction and stakeholder satisfaction—is a decisive success criterion that can either foster or hamper achieving success in terms of both client and stakeholder satisfaction. Therefore, an appropriate project implementation strategy is a key success factor, at least for the following reasons:

- Contrary to mass production, the buyer of the project result (i.e., the project client of an external project) needs to be involved in managing the implementation. Different types of contracts (see Chapter 10) impose different levels of involvement on the client in managing the implementation. At the same time, different clients have different project management capabilities both in terms of capacity and professionalism. Thus, from the point of view of achieving success both in terms of the project result and the duration time, the type of contract used in the project needs to be matched with the client's available project management capability.

- Different types of payment (see Chapter 11) impose different degrees of cost-related risks and responsibilities on both the client and the external contributor. Thus, from the point of view of achieving success in terms of the implementation cost, the allocated risks and responsibilities should be manageable for the parties involved. That is, the type of payment used in the project needs to be matched with the potential of the parties for managing the cost related risks and responsibilities.

- Projects that are considered to be successful in terms of the project triangle are more likely to elicit client satisfaction, and to foster stakeholder acceptance.

- The client needs to rely on the formulated project implementation strategy when the implementation phase of the project is contracted out since a contract should clearly outline the expectations of all parties. The bases of these expectations are implied in the predefined project implementation strategy.

However, in the course of formulating the appropriate project implementation strategy in the broader sense, there is a need for taking into account other factors (other than those highlighted in the first two bullet points). Consequently, a number of alternative project implementation strategies are available, and there is no single uniform solution. The issue of formulating appropriate project implementation strategy is discussed in Chapter 12.

The Scope of Formulating Project Implementation Strategy

The scope of formulating project implementation strategy implies:

- Making decisions on the type of contract and the type of payment, based on which a client organization intends to contract out the work;
- Making decisions on the type of tendering (and the implied prequalification), based on which a client organization creates possible competition for the potential external contributors; and
- Making decisions on the best bid, based on which the work to be contracted out is awarded to the external contributor.

These three decisions are strongly interrelated. Making decisions on the type of contract and the type of payment will determine making decisions on the type of tendering and the occasionally associated prequalification. Both the previously mentioned decisions have an impact—directly or indirectly—on identifying the best bid. Since the outcome of the first decision provides a basis for the subsequent decisions, it may be referred to as the narrow sense of project implementation strategy.

Chapter 10

Types of Contract

According to the approach adopted by the author, types of contract are the means by which the responsibilities and risks are allocated among the primary stakeholders in the project implementation process. These are the responsibilities and risks that are associated with the expected project result in its entirety and for the entire duration of the implementation phase. Thus, contract types are differentiated based on the extent to which a certain contractual arrangement shifts the majority of the above-mentioned responsibilities and risks onto the client or the external contributors.

The early literature (e.g., Thompson 1981; Perry 1985) does not clearly differentiate contract type from payment type. However, Thompson used two different terms for the two phenomena, namely contract systems (for types of contract) and types of contract (for types of payment). During the last two decades, authors (e.g., Bower, in Bower 2003b; Smith, in Smith 1995) gradually started to differentiate between contract type and payment type. However, the first phenomenon is referred to as organizational choice (Smith, in Smith 1995) or organizational structure (Bower, in Bower 2003b), while the second one is referred to as terms of payment (Smith, in Smith 1995) or payment mechanism (Bower, in Bower 2003b). Recently Marsh (in Turner 2009) introduced those principles by which he distinguished the types of contract (in his term: contract structures) in the context of construction projects. These principles imply:

- The responsibility for the entire implementation phase is placed with one single organization or it is divided among several external organizations.
- The contractor undertakes both managing the project and completing the work or is responsible for the management only, while the work is undertaken by other organizations.

The author of this book uses the term types of contract to introduce the allocation of responsibilities and risks that are associated with the expected project result as a whole and for the entire duration time of the implementation phase. According to the adopted approach, the author differentiates three basic types of contract. Thus, the types of contract are classified as traditional, turnkey, and management. Since the client is the primary stakeholder who needs to make decisions on the project implementation strategy applied in the project, this chapter provides an introduction to the three basic types of contract from the client's point of view. This introduction focuses on the inherent characteristics of the contract types. However, emphasis is also placed on those features which are characteristic of the types of contract, and that are derived from their inherent characteristics. Thus, a comparison of the types of contract is provided in detail at the end of this chapter.

The inherent characteristics of the contract types and their implied advantages and disadvantages will be utilized in the course of formulating the appropriate project implementation strategy.

Traditional Type of Contract

In traditional types of contract, work packages (at least two packages) are created from the work included in the project implementation phase. Then the client contracts out these work packages to different external contributors who are independent from each other in their contractual relationship to the client. Figure 10.1 shows the structure of the relationships characteristic of the primary stakeholders in a traditional contractual arrangement.

The outcome of completing a certain work package is a part of the expected project result (e.g., installing a booster station of a high pressure pipeline system), or the

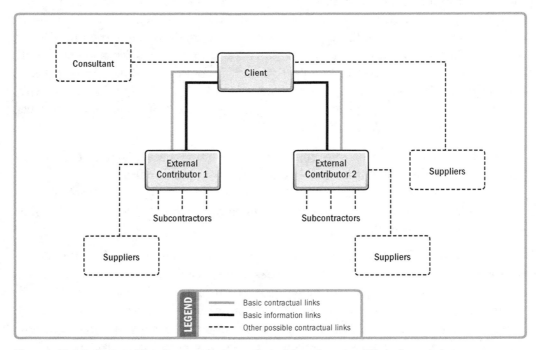

Figure 10.1 Relationships between the stakeholders in a traditional contract

outcome could provide a basis for bringing about a certain part of the project result (e.g., construction drawings). This type of contract implies that each external contributor takes responsibility and bears risks for only a certain part of the entire project result, and only for the associated part of the entire duration of implementation. The client needs to integrate these parts—according to the actual definition of the desired project result—as one coherent project result within the predefined time constraint. Consequently, the client is the primary stakeholder who needs to take and bear the majority of those responsibilities and risks that are associated with the expected project result as a whole and for the entire duration time of the implementation phase. That is, the majority of the above-mentioned responsibilities and risks are shifted onto the client organization.

Turnkey Type of Contract

The idea of the turnkey type of contract relies on a single external contributor to whom all the work in the implementation phase of the project is contracted out. This single external contributor is referred to as a turnkey contractor who has to take and bear the responsibilities and risks that are associated with the entire project result and for the whole duration of implementation. Figure 10.2 shows the structure of the relationships characteristic of the primary stakeholders in a turnkey contract.

The turnkey contractor may contract out several parts of the work to subcontractors. However, from the point of view of the client, this primary stakeholder is the only external contributor who needs to take and bear the responsibilities and risks,

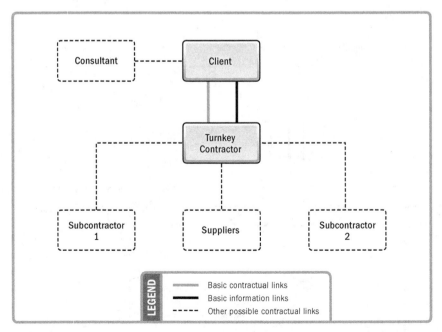

Figure 10.2 Relationships among the primary stakeholders in a turnkey contract

since the subcontractors are not in a contractual relationship with the client. Contrary to the traditional contract type, in the case of the turnkey type of contract, it is not the client but the external contributor—the turnkey contractor—who takes and bears the majority of the responsibilities and risks. These, from the point of view of the client, must not be shifted onto the subcontractors.

The turnkey type of contract, especially in the earlier construction project-related literature, is frequently referred to as a package deal system (Thompson 1981) or design-and-built contract (CIRIA SP 15 1981).

Management Type of Contract

Both in traditional and turnkey types of contract, there are two kinds of primary stakeholders, namely the client and the external contributor(s). As for the management contract, we find a third kind of primary player in the implementation phase of the project, who is referred to as a management contractor. The client of a project, in this case, may enter into a contract with an external project management organization, that is, the management contractor. The role of the management contractor is to provide project management services on behalf of the client. That is, management of the project implementation phase is a contractually defined separate issue. However, this stakeholder is not involved in the implementation process itself (i.e., the management contractor does not undertake any of the implementation). Figure 10.3

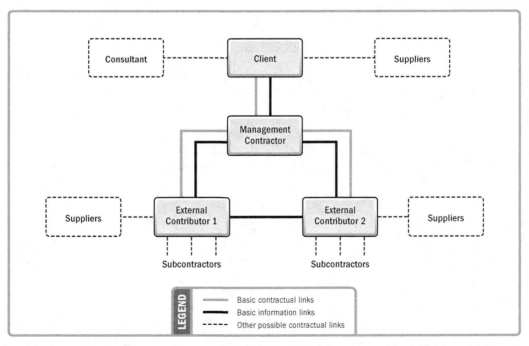

Figure 10.3 Relationships among the primary stakeholders in a management contract

shows the structure of the relationships characteristic of the primary stakeholders in a management contract.

Similar to the traditional type of contract, work packages are formed out of the work in the project implementation phase, and these work packages are contracted out to different external contributors. As part of project management services, the management contractor is responsible for formulating the work packages and for contracting them out, on behalf of the client, to those external contributors who complete the work. The management contractor is also responsible for controlling the work undertaken by the contributors, and for accepting and releasing payment for the completed work. Again, this stakeholder acts on behalf of the client.

In this way, the status of the management contractor is substantially different from the turnkey contractor's status. Since the management contractor is not involved in the implementation of the work, this stakeholder does not have a direct stake in this process. However, the management contractor has to take the responsibilities and to bear the risks that are associated with managing the project. At the same time, the management contractor acts similarly to an agent on behalf of the client. Thus, the client might not shift the majority of the responsibilities and risks onto the management contractor. However, from the point of view of the scope of responsibilities and risks, the management contractor provides project management services for the entire project implementation process. Thus, this stakeholder should accept a much broader scope of responsibilities and risks than those of the external contributors in a traditional contract. However, this wider scope of responsibilities and risks is directly associated with the professionalism of managing the project.

Taking into account the above considerations, one could say that in the case of a management contract, those responsibilities and risks that are associated with the expected project result as a whole and with the duration time of implementation are spread quite evenly among the primary stakeholders in comparison with the turnkey or traditional contract. That is why this type of contract is considered to be an intermediate alternative contract type between the turnkey and the traditional types of contract.

Table 10.1 summarizes the inherent characteristics of the types of contracts.

Table 10.1 The inherent characteristics of the contract types

Types of contracts	Duration time related majority of responsibilities and risks is shifted onto	Project result related majority of responsibilities and risks is shifted onto
Traditional	Client	Client
Turnkey	External contributor	External contributor
Management	Spread among the players	Spread among the players

A Comparison of the Types of Contract

So far, attention has been paid to the inherent characteristics of the three basic types of contracts. However, their different characteristics are decisive in identifying the appropriate project implementation strategy. Therefore, a comparison of the types of contracts is needed in order to highlight both their advantages and disadvantages. This comparison—adopting a client view again—is based on the following aspects that are drawn from previous research outcomes of the author (Görög 2007):

- Ambiguity of taking responsibility and bearing risk
- Potential for controlling the entire implementation phase in detail
- Potential for implementing changes during project implementation
- The flow of information between the external contributors
- The required project management capacity in the client organization
- The potential impact on the likely duration time of implementation
- The level of competition on the (potential) contractor side

In Chapter 12, a summary of the outcomes of the comparison is conceptualized in Table 12.1, while, the rest of this section goes into further detail.

Ambiguity of Taking Responsibility and Bearing Risk

When applying the turnkey type of contract, there is no ambiguity in the client organization regarding who should take and bear responsibility and risk when error is experienced in connection with the operation of the project result, or when faulty completion occurs during the implementation. On the other hand, the use of a traditional contract implies ambiguity because of the potential output-input relationship (pooled interdependence) of the work packages. In such a case, a hidden error in an earlier completed work package could lead to faulty completion in a subsequent package. However, both work packages belong to two different external contributors under the conditions of two different contracts. Therefore, identifying which of the external contributors should remedy the situation could be a real challenge. Because of the project management professionalism provided by the management contractor, the use of a management contract generally induces an in-between situation. However, calling the management contractor to account because of negligence is also a difficult matter.

Potential for Controlling the Entire Implementation Phase in Detail

In the case of work packages that are contracted out for external contributors to implement them, both traditional and management types of contract provide high potential for controlling the entire implementation process. However, in the case of management contracts, the control is undertaken by the management contractor instead of the client. Whereas, in the case of traditional contracts, control is undertaken directly by the client. The high potential for control is due to the fact that in case of these contract types, the client or the management contractor can overview the entire implantation process. However, from the point of view of the external contributors, the scope of control is limited by the boundaries of the work packages. Consequently, the client organization may exert influence on the implementation process to a great extent in both contract types.

At the same time, the use of a turnkey contract limits the client's potential for exercising control over the implementation process, since the turnkey contractor, by nature, can overview the implementation process. The limited control means that there is limited potential for influencing project implementation. However, unlike a management contractor, this stakeholder has a significant stake in the implementation process. In this way, the turnkey contractor can optimize its own outcome from the project instead of optimizing the client's outcome.

Potential for Implementing Changes During Project Implementation

Again, due to the work packages, both traditional and management types of contracts provide high potential for implementing changes during project implementation. This is due to the fact that different work packages are generally contracted out in accordance with the progress of the entire implementation process. However, the lower the number of work packages, the lower the potential for implementing changes easily. This potential also becomes lower and lower as the implementation process comes to an end. The use of the turnkey contract means a low potential for implementing changes easily since all the work encompassed by the entire implementation process are contracted out before commencing the implementation. In this way, the mode of implementing changes relies on the bargaining power of the parties involved.

The Flow of Information Among the External Contributors

Both traditional and management types of contract mean an indirect flow of information among the external contributors, that is, the client or the management contractor needs to mediate information among these players. If there is a need for intensive and time-consuming mediation of information, these conditions could lengthen the entire implementation process. However, the management contractors' project management professionalism could moderate this impact. The use of a turnkey contract makes a direct flow of information possible between the client and the turnkey contractor. However, when subcontractors are deployed, the turnkey contractor will face the same impact, unless he or she can moderate this impact through project management professionalism.

The Required Project Management Capacity in the Client Organization

It is clear that a client who uses a traditional type of contract needs to possess a considerable project management capacity and technical staff in order to cope with those responsibilities and risks that are shifted onto the client organization.

Lower-level project management capacity is required in the client organization when a turnkey contract is in use. The responsibilities and risks that are shifted onto the turnkey contractor necessitate this stakeholder taking over most of the management of the implementation phase of the project. However, there is no need for the client organization to possess considerable project management capacity in the case of a management contract, since a professional project management organization acts on behalf of the client who does not have a direct stake in the implementation process itself. Therefore, the management contractor can optimize the client's outcome from the project.

The Potential Impact on the Likely Duration Time of Implementation

When the entire project implementation phase is split up into work packages that are completed by different external contributors, the potential for utilizing overlaps between activities that belong to different packages (contributors) is very low. These conditions also could result in a longer implementation period in the case of both traditional and management contracts. However, the project management professionalism of the management contractor could moderate the consequences. At the same time, due to the single external contributor, a turnkey type of contract allows the use of potential overlaps to shorten the duration.

The Level of Competition on the Potential Contractor Side

Generally, there are more potential external contributors who can complete a work package that encompasses more or less homogeneous tasks than those who can undertake the entire implementation phase. Consequently, both traditional and management contracts encourage broader competition on the potential contractor side which, in itself, could lead to lower implementation cost. However, the turnkey type of contract can result in somewhat narrow competition, which generally results in higher implementation cost.

Chapter 11

Types of Payment

Types of payment are the means by which the risks and responsibilities that are associated with the implementation cost of a project are allocated among the primary stakeholders involved in implementation. Payment types are differentiated based on the extent to which a certain type of payment shifts the majority of the above-mentioned risks and responsibilities onto the client or the external contributors. Types of payment are then classified as price-based, cost-based, and target-based. Since the client is the stakeholder who needs to make decisions about the project implementation strategy applied in the project, this chapter provides an introduction to the three basic types of payment, again from the client's point of view. This introduction focuses on the inherent characteristics of the basic payment types, although some attention also will be paid to time- and material-based payment. Emphasis is also placed on those features that are characteristic of the types of payment, and that are derived from their inherent characteristics. Thus, a comparison of the types of payment is provided in detail at the end of this chapter. The inherent characteristics of the payment types and their implied advantages and disadvantages will also be used in the course of formulating an appropriate project implementation strategy.

Surprisingly, in comparison with contract types, there is an extensive literature on payments. However, both types of contract and types of payment are used equally in the external projects, and there can be no contract without one of them. In spite of the different views stated in previous literature, a mutually agreed interpretation of the concept is gradually emerging. In order to avoid ambiguity, the first section of this chapter is devoted to providing a brief overview of the different views on the phenomenon of payment.

Views on Payment

As it was pointed out in the previous chapter, the early literature (e.g., Thompson 1981; Perry 1985) does not differentiate clearly the phenomena of contract type and payment type. However, Thompson used two different terms for the two phenomena, namely contract systems (for types of contract) and types of contract (for types of payment), similarly to Wearne (1976). Hayes et al. (1987) also used the term types of contract for types of payment, and the authors differentiated price-based contract, cost-based-contract, and target contract. Lock (1968) in his seminal book used the term contract type for payment type throughout a good few of editions of the book (e.g., Lock 1992).

However, most British authors started to stop using the term contract type for payment type around the last millennium, while most U.S. authors continue the earlier practice. For example, Gido and Clements (1999), Fleming (2003), Schwalbe (2004), and also the *PMBOK® Guide* (Project Management Institute, 2008) consistently use the term contract type for payment type. Although, these authors provide a clear introduction of the different payment arrangements, these arrangements are referred to as contract types.

At the same time, the British literature, also around the last millennium, started to differentiate clearly between types of contract and types of payment. For example, both Smith (in Smith 1995) and Bower (in Bower 2003b) make a clear distinction between the two phenomena. However, the first phenomenon is referred to as organizational choice (Smith, in Smith 1995) or organizational structure (Bower, in Bower 2003b), while the second one is referred to as terms of payment (Smith in Smith, 1995) or payment mechanism (Bower, in Bower 2003). While Wearne (in Lawson et al. 1999) uses the terms types of contract and terms of payment in order to differentiate the two phenomena. In a recently published book, Marsh (in Turner, 2009) also uses two terms, namely contract structures for types of contract and contract prices for types of payment. Turner (in Turner 2009), similarly to Marsh, differentiates the phenomena of contract type and payment type, although the first one is referred to as contract structure, while the second one is referred to as payment form.

The author of this book uses the term types of payment to introduce allocating the responsibilities and risks that are associated with the implementation cost of an external project.

Price-Based Type of Payment

Price-based type of payment implies that the financial counter-value (i.e., the amount of money paid by a client for an external contributor) of the work completed by the external contributors is fixed in advance. The financial counter-value of the work might be predefined as one single amount of money (lump-sum price) or by means of unit prices/rates. In the latter case, the quantity of the actual completion is multiplied by the associated unit prices/rates to determine the amount of money to be paid. The lump-sum price covers the financial counter-value of the project work completed by a certain external contributor. Both in the case of lump-sum price and unit prices/rates regardless of the actual cost occurring in the contributor organization the predefined money is paid by the client. In this way, the majority of the risk and responsibility associated with the implementation cost is shifted onto the external contributor.

Cost-Based Type of Payment

In the cost-based type of payment, the client reimburses the actual direct costs incurred by the external contributor during the implementation of the work. Furthermore, beyond the direct cost, a so-called fee is paid by the client in order to cover the contributor's overhead costs and profit. The fee is defined either as a certain percentage of the actual direct costs or as one single amount of money. In this way, the majority of the financial counter-value of the works paid by the client is the reimbursement of the actual direct costs that is unknown in advance, whereas the majority of the risk and responsibility associated with the implementation cost is shifted onto the client organization. It is especially true when the direct cost plus percentage is in use.

Target-Based Type of Payment

The idea of target-based type of payment derives from the client's potential interest in connection with the project triangle. A client organization might be interested (especially in the case of a cost-based type of payment) in completing the project implementation at a lower level of cost than estimated. Similarly, the client might be interested in completing the project implementation earlier than planned. However, the client might also be interested in achieving a better project result according to specific parameters. In order to achieve these aims, the client organizations could deploy the so-called target-based types of payment, such as cost target, time target, and parameter target. If the targets are surpassed, then the external contributor could also increase his profit. That is, the client shares the surplus benefit gained as a result of improved achievement with the contributor. However, when the actual achievement is worse than the planned value, the client incurs some loss that is also shared with the contributor.

The size constraint of this book limits explaining in detail the different solutions to target-based types of payment. Nevertheless, the following figures (Figures 11.1 to 11.3) conceptualize consecutively the operational logic of introducing cost target, time target, and parameter target.

When a target-based type of payment is in use, we need to bear in mind that any of the target-based types of payment need to be combined with one of the previously introduced types of payment. It seems to be self-evident that cost target should be combined with cost-based type of payment since the concept of the cost target could not be interpreted in connection with the concept of price. On the other hand, both time target and parameter target better fit a price-based type of payment.

Based on the short description of target-based types of payment, it is conceivable that the application of a certain solution to a target-based type of payment could act as an incentive mechanism for the contributor organization. However, the alignment of motivations of all the primary stakeholders is strongly required. In this way, the

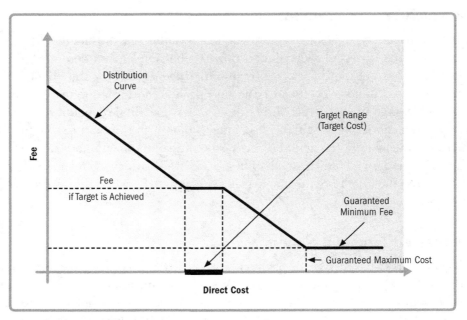

Figure 11.1 Operational logic of the cost target

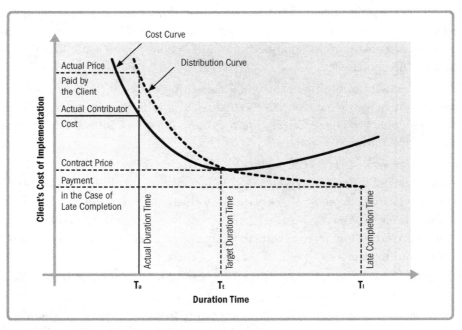

Figure 11.2 Operational logic of the time target

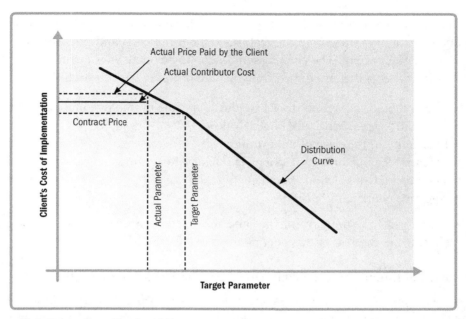

Figure 11.3 Operational logic of the parameter target

use of this type of payment results in a more balanced risk allocation in comparison either to pure price-based or pure cost-based type of payment. That is, the risk and responsibility that are associated with the project implementation cost are spread more evenly among the primary stakeholders.

Table 11.1 summarizes the inherent characteristics of the types of payment.

A Comparison of the Types of Payment

The previous parts of this chapter have been devoted to highlighting the inherent characteristics of the three basic types of payment, which are decisive when identifying the appropriate project implementation strategy. Therefore, a comparison of the types of payment is justified. In the course of comparing the types of payment, the focus is on price-based and cost-based types of payment. The reason behind this idea is that each target-based payment is applied in combination with the cost- or the price-based type

Table 11.1 The inherent characteristics of the payment types

Types of payment	Majority of the cost related responsibilities and risks are shifted onto
Price-based	External contributor(s)
Cost-based	Client
Target-based	Spread among the players

of payment. Hence, the target-based payments—because of their more balanced risk allocation capability—moderate the features of both the cost- and price-based type of payment to a great extent. The comparison—adopting a client view again—is based on the following aspects that are drawn from the author's previous research (Görög 2007):

- The potential impact on the likely duration time of implementation
- Potential for planning reliable cash-flow
- Flexibility in the case of uncertainty
- Potential for implementing changes during project implementation
- The potential impact on the payment mechanism
- Negative contributor attitude

In Chapter 12, a summary of the outcomes of comparison is conceptualized in Table 12.2, while the rest of this section goes into further detail.

The Potential Impact on the Likely Duration Time of Implementation

The use of a price-based type of payment necessitates a preliminary definition of the scope of work in order to make it possible for potential external contributors to create a realistic bid price. Such efforts are time-consuming, moreover, when the price-based type of payment is coupled with the traditional type of contract. There could be a need for time periods between the work packages because of their potential output-input relationship. This latter case could further lengthen the likely duration of project implementation. However, because of its opposite inherent characteristic, the cost-based type of payment might contribute to shortening the likely implementation time. The use of a cost-based type of payment does not necessitate predefining the work to be completed; consequently, it allows substantial overlaps even between the different work packages.

Potential for Planning Reliable Cash-flow

When a price-based type of payment is in use, the financial counter-value of the work completed by the external contributors is fixed in advance. As a result, the scope of work also needs to be known. As a result, the client—bearing in mind the time schedule and the terms of payment—is able to prepare a reliable cash-flow plan. A reliable cash-flow plan enables the client to use the money devoted to project implementation in the most economical manner. At the same time, the use of the cost-based type of payment does not presume a predefined scope of work. Therefore, due to its opposite inherent characteristic, the cost-based type of payment does not make the elaboration of a reliable cash-flow possible.

Flexibility in the Case of Uncertainty

When applying a price-based type of payment, the scope of work needs to be predefined, while the financial counter-value is fixed in some form or another. However, unforeseen events—uncertainties—could have a considerable impact on the implementation cost occurring in the contributor organization. These circumstances might lead to extreme contributor behavior during the bidding process that is manifested in two different ways, such as:

- A high bid price that could cover every potential unforeseen cost; or
- A low bid price to foster getting the project work.

Needless to say, the first attitude is disadvantageous for the client, since it may lead to an unjustified high contract price. However, the second one is also dangerous for the client since it could lead to permanent negative cash-flow balance for the project implementation on the contributor side. The permanent negative cash-flow balance, at the same time, hinders the proper implementation of the project work both in terms of quality and timely completion.

The reason for both kinds of extreme contributor behavior is the inflexibility characteristic of a price-based type of payment. At the same time, the cost-based type of payment is absolutely flexible when uncertainty occurs in the course of implementing the project. The flexibility of the cost-based type of payment is explained by the fact that it does not require defining the scope of work in advance. In addition, the client does not need to pay a fixed financial counter-value to the external contributor.

Potential for Implementing Changes During Project Implementation

Changes initiated by the client organization generally have a considerable impact on the implementation cost incurred by the contributor organization. Due to the inherent characteristic of the cost-based type of payment, changes are easily managed. Similarly, the use of unit prices/rates also provides a certain kind of mechanism for managing changes, since the basis of payment besides the unit prices/rates is the actually completed quantity of work. However, the use of the lump-sum price could create difficulties when changes occur. In the latter case, the impact of a change initiation on the amount of money to be paid for the external contributor heavily relies on the bargaining power of the parties. This could lead to unexpected consequences, such as lower quality, time overrun, etc.

The Potential Impact on the Payment Mechanism

The payment mechanism is the method by which proportional payments are defined. The use of a price-based type of payment might especially lead to an imbalanced payment mechanism. However, the two forms of this payment type could lead to imbalanced payment mechanism in different ways. When unit prices/rates are in use, during the bidding process the potential external contributors tend to overestimate the unit prices/rates of those activities that are completed at the beginning of implementation. Consequently, they tend to underestimate the later activities. In this way, a contributor can counterbalance the impact of the negative cash-flow balance period, while the client suffers from financial loss because of the time value of money. This is the so-called front-loaded mechanism.

The lump-sum price, however, could lead to an end-loaded payment mechanism. It occurs when the client breaks down the contract price in order to make the proportional payment possible. While doing so, the client tends to underestimate those activities that are completed at the beginning of implementation, and to overestimate the later activities. These circumstances result in lengthening the negative cash-flow balance period in the contributor organization in connection with the project work. The negative cash-flow balance might lead to financial difficulties in the course of implementing the project that, again, could hamper the implementation of the work.

At the same time, the use of a cost-based type of payment, again by nature, does not have an impact on the payment mechanism. since the reimbursement of the actual direct cost is the basis of the payment mechanism.

Negative Contributor Attitude

To a certain extent. both the price-based and the cost-based types of payment might engender from the point of view of the client some negative responses from the contributor. When using a pure price-based type of payment, the contributors work under the pressure of the price, whereas they need to limit the implementation cost to avoid loss that, when the price does not encompasses contingencies, could also hamper implementing the project execution both in terms of quality and duration. At the same time, the use of a pure cost-based type of payment may create an interest in the contributor organization in increasing direct cost in order to maximize returns at the expense of the client. The use of the direct cost plus percentage is a good case in point. These negative contributor responses characteristic of both price-based and cost-based types of payment are generally reinforced by using them in conjunction with a turnkey type of contract (see Chapter 10).

However, such negative contributor responses in the case of both pure price-based and pure cost-based types of payment show clearly that introducing some form of target-based payment could moderate their disadvantages.

Time and Material-Based Payment

This type of payment is a certain kind of combination of both the price-based and the cost-based types of payment which is often used in IS/IT projects. This payment type implies that the prices of supplies are fixed in advance either in terms of a single amount (lump-sum) or in terms of unit prices. At the same time, the payment for human services is based on some unit rate (e.g., hourly or weekly rates). Therefore, one could say that a time- and material-based payment is rather a combination of lump-sum and unit prices/rates. It seems to be true, however, that the quantity of human services may be open, and that is why this part of the payment could be considered to be cost-based instead. Consequently, the time- and material-based payment unify to a certain extent both the inherent characteristics and the derived features of both the price-based and cost-based types of payment.

Chapter 12

Formulating Appropriate Project Implementation Strategy in the Narrow Sense

The previous two chapters introduced the types of contract and the types of payment, and pointed out their inherent characteristics. The different contract and payment types both have advantages and disadvantages from the client organization's perspective. At the same time, not only the types of contract and the types of payment are different, but projects are also different, and they are implemented in different organizational contexts characteristic of the client organizations. The right use of project implementation strategy in the narrow sense means matching a certain type of contract and a certain type of payment to both the project characteristics and the client characteristics. This chapter addresses this issue of matching. Before doing so, both those project characteristics and client characteristics that are relevant from the point of view of matching will be highlighted. This is followed by a summary of those advantages and disadvantages (highlighted in detail in Chapter 10 and Chapter 11) that are characteristic of both types of contract and types of payment. These features might also be considered when matching project implementation strategy in the narrow sense with tendering and prequalification (see Chapter 14).

Approaches to Project Implementation Strategy

The existing literature on project implementation strategy may be grouped into two main branches. However, regardless of the approach adopted by the authors, the term contract strategy is used in this literature. One of the branches may be referred to as a non-systematic approach, which encompasses two further sub-branches. The other branch of project implementation strategy may be referred to as the systematic approach.

Non-Systematic Approach to Project Implementation Strategy

The first sub-branch of the non-systematic approach to project implementation strategy appeared in the early literature (e.g., Thompson 1981; Perry 1985). This approach does not differentiate clearly the phenomena of contract type from payment type; however, suggestions are made regarding their use. At the same time, Thompson (in Wearne 1989) draws the attention to the importance of making decisions on contract (project implementation) strategy. He emphasized that this decision affects the responsibilities of the parties, and also the risks borne by the parties. In addition, the selected strategy greatly influences both the level and forms of client involvement in managing the implementation of the project.

Another sub-branch of the non-systematic approach appeared in the literature over the last two decades (e.g., Bower, in Bower 2003b; Smith, in Smith 1995). This sub-branch differentiates the phenomena of contract type and payment type. However, the first phenomenon is referred to as organizational choice (Smith, in Smith 1995) or organizational structure (Bower, in Bower 2003b) while the second one is referred to as terms of payment (Smith, in Smith 1995) or payment mechanism (Bower, in Bower 2003b). Similarly to Thompson (in Wearne 1989), Smith also emphasizes that the responsibilities of the parties should be determined while the associated risks need to be allocated among the parties. Bower goes further when she states that in the course of selecting contract (project implementation) strategy, the client needs to decide the relative importance of duration time, implementation cost, and the quality of performance of the completed project result. She also emphasizes that the contract (project implementation) strategy needs to balance incentive, flexibility, and risk sharing.

Systematic Approach to Project Implementation Strategy

Recently Turner (in Turner 2009) developed a systematic approach to selecting implementation strategy, although he also uses the term contract strategy. Turner differentiates the phenomena of contract type and payment type, although the first one is referred to as contract structure, while the second one is referred to as payment form in his book. Based on his research, Turner elaborated a selection method based on a twofold aim, that is, the contract (project implementation) strategy should contribute to developing a cooperative project organization and to allocating the management of risk in an appropriate manner.

Turner states in his book that different contract structures (types of contract) naturally attract the form of payment (types of payment) selected previously; therefore, he places considerable emphases on selecting the payment type. Turner suggests a selection methodology that is primarily based on which primary stakeholder controls the risk (client, contractor, or both). The potential for controlling the risk depends on where the risk lies (in the project result, the implementation process, or both). According to Turner's approach, the contractor (external contributor) can control the risk best when the risk itself lies in the project implementation process. However, if the risk lies in the project result—which implies risk also in the project implementation process—both the client and the contractor need to control the risk. However, the risk could also lie in the final purpose of the client (that needs to be achieved by means of the project result), which necessitates the client's control over the risk.

Taking together the need for a cooperative project organization that requires goal alignment among the players and the best potential for controlling the risk associated with the project, Turner suggests the following use of contract strategy:

- When both the expected project result and the underlying purpose of the client are properly defined, the use of a price-based contract is justified
- When the expected project result is uncertain, or when the underlying client's purpose might undergo changes, the use of a cost-based contract is needed

Turner, also taking into consideration the level of complexity characteristic of a project, further elaborates his selection methodology regarding the right use of the different payment forms (types of payment), and he points out the contract structure (type of contract) that is naturally attracted by a certain payment form.

The author of this book, based on his previous research (Görög 2007) and experience gained from consultancy, also developed a systematic method (that is further developed here) of formulating an appropriate project implementation strategy in the narrow sense. The selection method is based on the following assumptions:

- Projects as temporary phenomena are different due to the extent to which they comprise the inherent project characteristics
- Project clients are different, either in terms of the relative importance of duration time, implementation cost, and the quality of performance of the completed project result, or in terms of their project management professionalism (i.e., the extent to which they might be able to manage the implementation phase of the project in an efficient manner)
- None of the types of contract is better than another, however, due to their different nature they have different inherent characteristics
- None of the types of payment is better than another; however, due to their different nature, they have different inherent characteristics

The author's aim is to introduce a method of identifying project implementation strategy that results in matching the inherent characteristics of both the applied contract and payment type, as well as the inherent characteristics of the project and the client. In this way, both those risks and responsibilities that are associated with implementing the project are allocated in an appropriate manner (in accordance with the primary stakeholders' ability to manage risk and responsibility). Consequently, there will be a potential for a higher level of cooperation between the client and the external contributors, instead of each trying to outdo the other.

Although there is potential for integrating the two systematic approaches to selecting project implementation strategy, this aim is outside of the scope of this book.

The following section of the book will highlight the inherent characteristics of projects and those of client organizations, followed by a summary of the inherent characteristics of both the types of contracts and types of payment. Then, based on matching the highlighted characteristics, an implementation strategy formulation method will be introduced.

Projects and Clients—Their Inherent Characteristics

In this part of the chapter, we focus on those project and client characteristics that are considered to be inherent characteristics, and that need to be considered when a client organization is busy formulating the most appropriate project implementation strategy for an external project.

Project Characteristics

The Tavistock Institute (1966) identified two inherent characteristics of projects, *uncertainty and interdependence*.

Uncertainty might be experienced in a project due to:

- Novelty regarding either the desired project result or the work process that brings about the project result. The higher the novelty either in the expected project result or the implementation process, the lower the potential for defining the scope of work to be done in an appropriate manner, and, consequently, the lower the potential for predicting the resource demand, the duration, and the likely implementation cost.
- Availability of relevant information regarding the context for implementing the project. The lower the level of available information or relevant information (i.e., the higher the level of uncertainty), again, the lower the potential for properly defining the scope of work to be done, and, consequently, the lower the potential for predicting the resource demand, the duration, and the likely implementation cost.
- The level of clarity regarding the definition of the desired project result. The higher the level of uncertainty as to the desired project result, the lower the potential for properly defining the scope of work to be done, and, consequently, the lower the potential for predicting the resource demand, the duration, and the likely implementation cost.
- Ambiguity characteristic of legislation and inflation. The higher the ambiguity (i.e., the uncertainty), the lower the potential for predicting the likely duration and the implementation cost.

Interdependence as mutual interrelationship implies:

- Complexity of the workflow interdependence, that is, how the project tasks depend on each other in the course of implementation (the higher the level of uncertainty, the higher the complexity of workflow interdependence). The higher the complexity of the workflow interdependence, the higher the required efficiency to coordinate the project implementation process.

- Complexity of the operational process, that is, how the operability of the different parts of the desired project result depend on each other in the course of operation. The higher the complexity of the operational process of the expected project result, the higher the need for integrating the implementation process (including tests).

Client Characteristics

When client organizations have to match project implementation strategy in the narrow sense with the client's inherent characteristics, these can differ in two ways:

- The available project management professionalism, both in terms of capacity (number of people), and expertise and experience. The lower the level of available project management professionalism in the client organization, the lower the potential for managing the implementation phase of the project in an efficient manner.
- The level of relative importance of cost saving, earlier completion, and better performance parameters of the expected project result. The higher the level of the relative importance of one of them, the higher the need for implementing the associated incentive mechanism in the course of implementing the project.

Types of Contracts and Types of Payment: Their Inherent Characteristics

Different features of the types of contracts and the types of payment and their underlying inherent characteristics of them were highlighted in the previous two chapters; however, providing a summary of these features seems to be useful again here. Table 12.1 and Table 12.2 provide an overview of the salient features of the types of contract and the types of payment respectively.

Matching Project Implementation Strategy with the Inherent Characteristics of the Project and Those of the Client

Bearing in mind the features and the inherent characteristics discussed earlier, we need to consider using them in formulating an appropriate project implementation strategy in the narrow sense. An appropriate project implementation strategy implies that both types of contract and types of payment match both project characteristics and client characteristics in order to manage risk and responsibility appropriately, and to foster cooperation among the primary stakeholders of the project implementation

Table 12.1 Characteristics of the types of contract

Aspects of the Comparison	Types of Contract		
	Traditional	Turnkey	Management
The majority of responsibilities and risks (the entire project result and the entire duration time) shifted onto	Client	Contributor	Spread between the players
Ambiguity of taking responsibility and bearing risk	Potential for high ambiguity	No ambiguity	Low ambiguity
Potential for controlling the entire implementation phase in detail	High potential	Low potential	High potential
Potential for implementing changes during the project implementation	High potential	Low potential	High potential
The flow of information between the external contributors	Indirect	Direct	Moderate indirect
The required project management capacity in the client organization	Substantially high	Moderate	Low
The potential impact on the likely duration time of implementation	Lengthens the duration time	Shortens the duration time	Moderately lengthens the duration time
The level of competition on the potential contractor side	Broad	Narrow	Broad

Table 12.2 Characteristics of the types of payment

Aspects of the Comparison	Types of Payment		
	Price-Based	Cost-Based	Target-Based
The majority of risks and responsibilities (implementation cost) is shifted onto	Contributor	Client	Spread between the players
The potential impact on the likely duration time of implementation	Lengthens the duration time	Shortens the duration time	In-between; determined by the underlying payment
Potential for planning reliable cash flow	High potential	Low potential	In-between; determined by the underlying payment
Flexibility in case of uncertainty	No flexibility	High flexibility	In-between; determined by the underlying payment
Potential for implementing changes during the project implementation	Lump-sum: low potential; unit/prices/rates: moderate potential	High potential	In-between; determined by the underlying payment
The potential impact on the payment mechanism	Imbalanced payment mechanism	No impact on the payment mechanism	Determined by the underlying payment
Negative contractor attitude	Tends to lowering quality	Tends to increase direct cost	Moderates contractor attitude

process. According to the author's experience, a wide variety of combinations of types of contract and types of payment are available; however, the author cannot discuss all possible combinations. Instead, the aim is to highlight the main points for those who are responsible for developing a project implementation strategy in the narrow sense for external projects.

Types of payment are the tools by means of which those risks and responsibilities are allocated among the primary stakeholders who are associated with the implementation cost of a project. In order to find the appropriate payment type, first one of the inherent project characteristics (i.e., the level of uncertainty) needs to be taken into consideration. Based on the level of uncertainty, one can identify whether price-based or cost-based type of payment is appropriate.

Low level of uncertainty is favorable for using a price-based type of payment, as the scope of work to be completed may be defined precisely, consequently the potential external contributors (the bidders) are able to estimate both the resource demand and the likely duration time of implementation. In this way, they are able to estimate the likely implementation cost, and consequently, they are able to specify a reliable bid price (either lump-sum or unit prices/rates).

In the case of high level uncertainty, the wise client uses a cost-based type of payment. What will happen if the client applies a price-based type of payment when the project contains a high level of uncertainty? In such a situation—since the scope of work could not be predicted properly—the potential external contributors (the bidders) are not able to define resource demand and duration time properly. If they are not able to estimate the implementation costs precisely, they are not able to specify a suitable bid price. Finally, the inflexibility characteristic of a price-based type of payment could lead to extreme bidding behavior (see Chapter 11).

The relationship between the level of uncertainty and the appropriate type of payment as it is highlighted above is conceptualized in Figure 12.1.

The viability of applying any target-based arrangement necessitates considering the other client characteristics. Here, the relative importance of cost saving, earlier completion, and better performance parameters of the expected project result need to be evaluated. If these elements are important to the client, then he or she should analyze whether the required target-based arrangement is compatible with the chosen type of payment. Potential for combining price-based or cost-based payment types with target mechanism are also discussed in Chapter 11.

Types of contract are the tools by means of which those risks and responsibilities are allocated among the players who are associated with the expected project result as a whole and the entire duration time of implementing the project. In order to find the appropriate contract type, we need to take into account one of the inherent project characteristics—that is, the level of complexity—and one of the client characteristics—that is, the available project management professionalism in

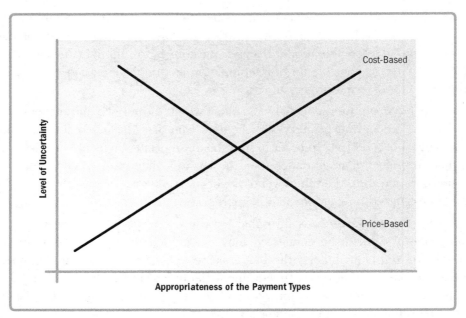

Figure 12.1 The relationship between the level of uncertainty and the appropriateness of the payment types

the client organization. Based on the level of complexity and the level of available project management professionalism, one can identify whether a traditional or turn-key type of contract or a management contract is appropriate.

In the case of low complexity of both the workflow and the operational process interdependence, the potential advantages of a traditional type of contract could be utilized if the client possesses the required project management professionalism. When the client does not possess this professionalism there is no potential for exercising efficient coordination and control over the implementation process. Consequently, the client could not use the advantages of the traditional type of contract, however, its disadvantages will become especially prominent.

High complexity of workflow interdependence (e.g., reciprocal relationships between tasks when developing an unusual product) requires intensive mediation of information among external contributors when using a traditional type of contract. Without well-established project management professionalism, a client organization could not cope with managing the project implementation process in an efficient way. Thus, implementing the project will result in both time and cost overrun. In order to minimize the potential for time and cost overrun in such a case, depending on the available project management professionalism in the client organization, the wise client tends to apply a turnkey or management type of contract. The lower the level of available project management professionalism, the stronger the need for using a management contract.

For high complexity of the operational process (i.e., when the operability of the different parts of the desired project result heavily depends on other parts in the course of the operational phase of the completed project result), a turnkey type of contract is required. What will happen if the client applies a traditional type of contract in such a situation? We need to bear in mind that, generally speaking, the outcome of a certain work package is only one part of the whole project result. Due to the complexity of the operational process interdependence, the client is not able, even if the client or a hired agency possesses the required professionalism, to test and prove the proper operability of these parts. In such a case, those risks and responsibilities that are associated with the project result as a whole and the entire duration of implementing the project need to be integrated in one single external contributor organization.

The relationship between the level of complexity and the appropriate type of contract as highlighted above is conceptualized in Figure 12.2. The relationship between the level of available professionalism and the appropriate type of contract as highlighted above is conceptualized in Figure 12.3.

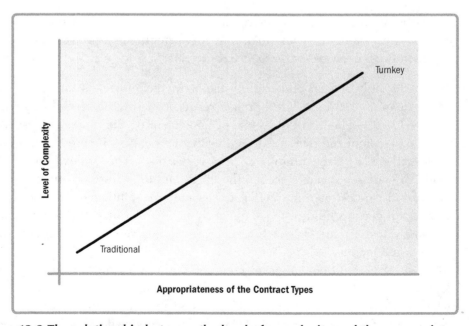

Figure 12.2 The relationship between the level of complexity and the appropriateness of the contract types

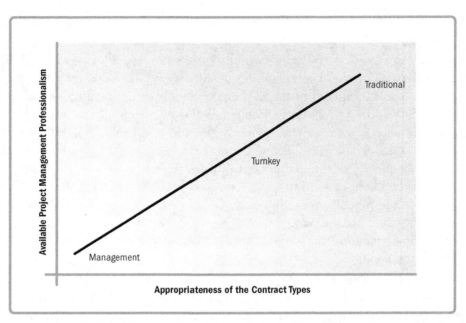

Figure 12.3 The relationship between the level of available PM professionalism and the appropriateness of the contract types

Besides the main points highlighted earlier, project managers also need to consider the following potential issues when they are formulating a project implementation strategy in the narrow sense for external projects:

- When the only serious uncertainty factor in the project is either the weak scope definition of the desired project result or the high potential for changes initiated by the client in the course of implementing the project, the scope of work to be completed by the external contributor cannot be predicted. In such a case, the use of the lump-sum price—because of its inflexibility—could result in endless debates between the client and the external contributor. The use of unit prices/rates may offer a reasonable resolution in such a case. It provides a certain kind of mechanism by means of which the actual amount of money to be paid for the external contributor can be determined in an appropriate manner.

- The use of a traditional type of contract limits utilizing the potential overlaps between those project activities that belong to different contributors, whereas this type of contract could lengthen the entire duration of the project. This unfavorable impact could be moderated considerably if a traditional type of contract is suitably combined with a cost-based type of payment. The flexibility characteristic of the cost-based type of payment may lessen the cumbersome nature of the traditional type of contract from the point of view of utilizing overlaps, since the use of a cost-based type of payment does not necessitate defining precisely the scope of work to be completed.

- The use of a turnkey type of contract, at the same time, limits implementing changes in the course of project implementation. The cumbersome nature of a turnkey type of contract might also be counterbalanced by means of combining a turnkey contract and a cost-based type of payment, since the latter is very flexible regarding changes. However, the use of unit prices/rates could also moderate the above-mentioned impact of a turnkey type of contract to a certain extent.

- When using a lump-sum price, the consequences of changes initiated by the client relies on the bargaining power of the primary stakeholders, as it was pointed out in an earlier chapter. Combining the lump-sum price and the traditional type of contract (when the use of the latter is justified) may counterbalance this kind of inflexibility characteristic of the lump-sum price, since the use of work packages means a higher potential for implementing changes to the desired project result.

The likelihood of these above-mentioned potential situations is supported by the typical characteristics of both contract and payment types, and can decrease their mutual disadvantages to a certain extent.

Case Examples of the Formulation of Appropriate Project Implementation Strategies in the Narrow Sense

Real Estate Development Project

The aim of the project was to construct a new building complex to provide residence for senior citizens, and, at the same time, to provide possibilities for leisure-time activities and for everyday medical care. Accordingly, the desired project result— the building complex—encompassed a residence block, a medical block, library, swimming pool, and a service block. The client organization of the project has been involved in the real estate development business for many years. However, the client does not have either designing or construction capacity, thus they have to rely on external contributors when new projects emerge. Therefore, after outlining the scope of the desired project result (with the help of a hired architect consultant), including the associated capacity and quality requirements, the client started to formulate the project implementation strategy in the narrow sense. The project included the construction design and the construction work itself, including all those activities that are needed to create an operable building complex according to the predefined values, and within the specified time constraint.

Before making a decision on the project implementation strategy, the client evaluated the level of uncertainty and the complexity of interdependence characteristic to the project. The outcomes of the analysis were as follows:

- The desired project result is defined clearly, and there is no potential for serious changes during the project implementation.
- The desired project result utilizes time-tested solutions, while the work process that brings about the project result relies on time-tested technologies.
- The construction site is considered to be known since all the important information is available.
- Legislation that could have an impact on the project result and on the implementation process is unambiguous and foreseeable. However, the inflation rate is not negligible but it seems to be stable, and sudden changes are not expected.
- Due to the low level of uncertainty, the analysis has not revealed any potential for complex workflow interdependence (i.e., each part of the building complex is likely to be constructed as it is designed). Furthermore, there is no potential for complex operational process interdependence, since the operability of the different parts of the building complex does not depend on each other in the course of the operation.

The project client also analyzed its own organization, and they found that:

- The client possesses not only the required technical staff (sufficient number of construction engineers) but there is considerable project management professionalism (sufficient number of trained and experienced project managers), as well. However, their previous projects were less complex.
- Because of the expectations of the owners of the client organization, there is a salient need for cost saving.

Taking into account the above conditions, the client formulated the following project implementation strategy: a traditional type of contract (work packages for construction and installation design, civil engineering construction, and building engineering installation), and a lump-sum price for each work package. Since the desired project result was defined clearly and there was no potential for serious changes during the project implementation, there was no need for unit prices/rates to manage the impact of changes. The client, in order to save costs, at first wanted to apply a cost-based type of payment in order to make it possible to introduce a cost target. Finally, before making the final decision, they understood that there was no potential for cost saving due to the very low level of uncertainty. Therefore, it was possible for the bidders (the potential external contributors) to define the resource demand of the work, and consequently, they were able to undertake a precise cost assessment, based on which giving a reliable bid price was also possible. The client understood that in such a situation, and because of the likely strong competition, there was no potential for achieving cost saving in the course of the implementation.

The owners of the client accepted this decision since they understood that introducing cost target (and the underlying cost-based type of payment) is counterproductive in the case of low level uncertainty.

Information System Project

The client organization of this project was a furniture manufacturer company which bought out a few similar companies in Central Europe in the late 1990s. These companies used different planning and controlling systems, which proved to be a hindrance to the operational efficiency. Therefore, the underlying strategic objective of the project was to increase the operational efficiency and to lower the company overhead cost. The aim of the project was the implementation of an enterprise resource planning (ERP) system. The new ERP system was expected to encompass all the functional processes in each company owned by the client organization.

When the decision was made, the client invited three external contributors to submit their tender bid on a time and material basis. The project implementation was contracted out in the frame of a turnkey contract to the cheapest-price bidder. Since the client organization was neither experienced in project management nor in the expected information system, the project implementation process very soon became a disaster. There was no real progress on the project, but the client had to pay the time-related fee to the contributor. After a few months, and after paying out a considerable amount of money, the client decided to dissolve the contract. However, the client did not want to cancel the project itself. Therefore, an independent project management consultant was hired to assist the client organization in reconsidering the entire project implementation.

It was agreed that an appropriate project implementation strategy would be the key to completing the project successfully. First the consultant and the management team of the client evaluated the level of uncertainty and the complexity of interdependence characteristic of the project. The outcomes of their analysis are summarized as follows:

- The need for the project result is defined clearly; however, the desired project result itself is not defined at all. In addition, the client is not able to define the scope of the expected project result.
- The desired project result seems to be time-tested (box off the shelf software package). However, the work process that brings about the project result could involve considerable uncertainties because of the likely unknown customization.

- The project implementation site (i.e., operational process of the client organization) is unknown to the potential external contributors.
- Legislation that could have an impact on the project result and on the implementation process is unambiguous and foreseeable. The inflation rate is low and stable, and unforeseeable sudden changes are not expected.
- Because of the high level of uncertainty, the analysis revealed a high potential for complex workflow interdependence, that is, a high potential for rework. However, there is also potential for complex operational process interdependence since the operability of the different functions of the desired ERP system is highly dependent on each other.

The consultant and the client's team also analyzed the client organization, and the following characteristics were found:

- The client organization is inexperienced both in project management, and in using and operating the expected information system.
- There is no need for better achievement in terms of the implementation cost, the duration time, and performance parameters in the client organization. However, the associated values need to be fixed before contracting out the implementation work.

Taking into account all of the above conditions, the consultant and the client's team came to an agreement regarding the project implementation strategy in the narrow sense to be applied in this project. The use of a management type of contract was decided. The use of a management type of contract also meant formulating work packages that were contracted out to different external contributors. As part of the project management services, the management contractor was responsible for formulating these work packages and also for contracting them out, on behalf of the client, to those external contributors who will complete them.

Since the management type of contract was decided upon, the type of payment was also considered from the point of view of the management contractor. It required the assessment of the likely duration time of the entire project implementation process. In order to achieve this end, an independent IT/IS consultant, experienced in similar projects, was involved in the decision-making team. The joint effort resulted in a reliable prediction of the likely duration time of the whole project, which justified the use of the price-based (lump-sum) type of payment in the client-management contractor relationship.

Finally, the project was completed successfully, which meant that the chosen project implementation strategy was justified.

Chapter 13

Tendering and Prequalification

After making a decision on project implementation strategy in the narrow sense, the client of an external project needs to select one or more external contributors to implement the project work. The toolkit for selecting contributors from among the potential contributors is tendering, and occasionally an associated prequalification. While tendering is a kind of competitive bidding, prequalification is a preliminary evaluation of the potential external contributors, based on a predefined set of criteria, before entering into the tendering phase. The outcome of making decisions on project implementation strategy in the narrow sense has a considerable impact on the use of both tendering and prequalification. However, this interrelationship will be discussed in the next chapter. In this chapter we turn our attention to introducing the most frequently used types of tendering, and to highlighting the aim, and process of prequalification. Emphasis is now placed on the technical aspects of the two phenomena. This chapter will focus more on the phenomenon of prequalification for two reasons: (a) existing literature on prequalification, contrary to literature on tendering, is rather weak, (b) the applied project implementation strategy in the narrow sense has a more direct impact on the use of prequalification.

Types of Tendering

One of the earlier works that provides an extensive overview on tendering is the book written by Marsh (1981), who differentiated the kinds of tendering in connection with the bid price. Marsh identified four solutions (they were referred to as methods in Marsh's book): (a) open tendering for the whole contract price; (b) selective tendering for the whole contract price; (c) selective tendering for unit prices/rates; and (d) negotiation with a single potential contributor for the whole contract price.

Smith (in Smith 1995) considered tendering as a procedure by means of which a client can select external contributors for implementing project work. Smith differentiated among:

- Competitive tendering that may be either open or selective;
- Two stage tendering, where the final bid is developed from cost and price data supplied with the initial competitive bid;

- Negotiated tendering with 1 to 3 potential contributors;
- Continuity tendering, which implies that similar projects will be awarded to the winner based on the original bid;
- Serial tendering, where bidders enter into a series of contracts; and
- Term tendering, where the type of work is known but the amount of work is unknown and the time period of the contract is fixed.

However, tendering is not just a procedure but a competition as well in order to identify the most appropriate bidder as external contributor, and to enter into a contract with this organization. Although there are a few different solutions for selecting external contributors, this chapter is going to consider those most frequently used tendering arrangements that rely on competition.

From the point of view of combining (i.e., matching tendering and prequalification with the applied project implementation strategy in the narrow sense), the author differentiates types of tendering based on how the prequalification itself relates to the tendering. Therefore, this chapter encompasses:

- Open tendering;
- Selective tendering;
- Two-tier tendering; and
- Invitation tendering.

The reader of this book might realize that the above-listed types of tendering show a similarity both to Marsh's (1981) and to Smith's (1995) typology introduced earlier. However, we need to bear in mind that both these typologies were considered within the context of construction projects. The author of this book interprets the types of tendering but without focusing on the physical nature of the project result. Since the readers of this book may be familiar with the fundamentals of these types of tendering, only their relationships with prequalification will be highlighted here.

Open tendering does not require prequalification, thus each potential contributor can submit a tender bid. Contrary to the open tender, when using *selective tendering*, only those potential external contributors may submit their tender bids who have been prequalified for the project work in question. Selective tendering implies that bidding is preceded by prequalification.

As for *two-tier tender*, we need to differentiate at least two solutions, such as two-step and two-stage systems. However, it is common for both solutions that a certain part of the tender bid is coupled with the prequalification itself. In the case of two-step tendering, a proposal for the technical solution of the desired project result (or the problem to be solved by means of a project result) is submitted along with prequalification, while in the case of two-stage tendering, unit prices/rates are submitted along with prequalification.

Invitation tendering implies that a client invites a few potential external contributors to submit their tender bid. Similar to the open tender, bidding is not preceded

Table 13.1 Relationship between tendering and prequalification

Types of Tendering	Prequalification
Open tendering	No prequalification
Selective tendering	Bidding is preceded by prequalification (only prequalified external contributors may submit bid)
Two-tier tendering Two-step system	Proposal for the technical solution and prequalification precedes bidding
Two-stage system	Proposal for unit prices/rates and prequalification precedes bidding
Invitation tendering Direct invitation	No prequalification, invitation is based on unique know-how
Serial tendering	No prequalification, invitation is based on previous experience

by prequalification; however, only those who have been invited can submit a bid. An invitation tender may be based on a direct invitation (e.g., because of the unique know-how of a few potential external contributors) or may be based on a so-called serial tender (e.g., a client wants to implement the same project a few times but in different locations, or a complex information system project will be implemented in a stage-by-stage manner).

Table 13.1 summarizes the relationship between tendering and prequalification highlighted above.

The Aim and the Process of Prequalification

Prequalification is a preliminary evaluation of the potential external contributors based on a predefined set of criteria in order to identify those potential contributors who are capable of implementing the project work. Because of the nature of the project business, external contributors, instead of selling an already-completed product, need to sell their capability of completing projects that result in the expected outcome. At the same time, clients need to rely on the external contributors to a considerable extent in the course of implementing the project. The extent to which a client needs to rely on external contributors primarily depends on the applied project implementation strategy in the narrow sense. Thus, the client organizations should identify those potential contributors who are considered to be reliable. A formal way of evaluating potential contributors is prequalification which – due to the previously mentioned nature of the project business – is a multi-faceted phenomenon.

Different authors suggest different lists of criteria based on what potential external contributors need to be evaluated before bidding (e.g., El-Sawalhi, Eaton, and

Rustom, 2007). However, Bower (in Bower 2003c) and Görög (2003) considered prequalification in a more systematic manner. Accordingly, a farsighted prequalification of potential contributors needs to consider:

- Technical capability (i.e., familiarity and skill regarding the technical—in the wider sense of the term—components of the expected project result and that of the implementation process, and the available capacity to do the project);
- Financial capability (i.e., a solid financial background based on which a contributor organization is able to manage both the risk associated with the implementation cost and the consequences of the so-called negative cash-flow balance period of implementing the project); and
- Project management capability (i.e., sufficient project management professionalism by means of which a contributor organization is able to plan and control implementing the project).

Besides these basic aspects of prequalification, the context of a given project may necessitate considering other contributor characteristics, such as: health and safety systems, familiarity with the locality of the project (including the operational context of the expected project result), and so forth. The author is going to pay attention to the above-listed three main aspects of contributor capability, as the use of them, unlike other potential criteria, is closely connected to the applied project implementation strategy in the narrow sense.

The client organizations need to collect information regarding all the three aspects of the contributor capability. In doing so, a client could rely on well-established standard forms, such as Standard Prequalification Form for Contractors (by Fédération Internationale des Ingénieurs Conseils) or Standard Prequalification Questionnaires and Financial Statement for Bidders (by The Associated General Contractors of America). These forms can be customized to the actual project context.

Technical capability needs to be evaluated at least in terms of the following criteria:

- Resources available for the project (human resources, plants, subcontractors, and suppliers), and the work in progress of the applicants
- References regarding successfully completed similar projects
- Quality assurance regarding the project tasks
- Familiarity with and experience in working in accordance with the required technical specifications

Financial capability is reliably evaluated by means of the following criteria:

- Balance sheets
- Profit and loss statements

- Evaluating creditability (by means of bank reference)
- Financial liability insurance policy

Project management capability might be evaluated in terms of the following criteria:

- References regarding successfully completed projects, based on the same type of contract
- Project management expertise
- Quality assurance regarding managing projects
- Organizational arrangement both at company level and project level, and the reporting relationship between the two levels (These conditions considerably determine the length of an external contributor's reaction time that may be decisive when a client initiates changes in the course of project implementation. Thus, organizational arrangement is also considered to be, at least an indirect project management capability.)

The capability aspects and the associated decisive criteria are summarized in Table 13.2.

Table 13.2 Capability aspects and the associated evaluation criteria

Capability Aspects of Prequalification	Evaluation Criteria
Technical capability	Available resources (human, plants, subcontractors, suppliers)
	Quantity of work in progress
	References (similar projects)
	Quality assurance (work)
	Familiarity with specifications
Financial capability	Balance sheet
	Profit and loss statement
	Creditability
	Financial liability insurance
Project management capability	References (same contract type)
	Project management expertise (professionals)
	Quality assurance (project management)

	Organizational arrangement
	    company level
	    project level
	    reporting relationship

Probably the most salient step in prequalifying potential external contributors is the evaluation itself that results in distinguishing all capable potential external contributors. Bearing in mind the scoring point evaluation system and the associated nominal scale to score applicants, the process of evaluation includes:

- Ranking the three aspects of capability according to their order of importance;
- Ranking the criteria belonging to the aspects of capability;
- Weighting the criteria in accordance with their rank;
- Devising an evaluation scale for each criterion;
- Evaluating each applicant against each criterion;
- Identifying all capable potential contributors.

Both kinds of ranking, then weighting and devising the associated evaluation scale, are strongly linked to the previously formulated project implementation strategy in the narrow sense. Thus, these issues will be discussed and illustrated further in the following chapter. However, it is necessary to highlight the steps listed above.

The next chapter will discuss, among other themes, the impact of project implementation strategy in the narrow sense on the use of prequalification. These implications of project implementation strategy will determine the importance of each capability aspect, and consequently will affect the importance of those criteria that belong to the capability aspects. That is, not only the three capability aspects but also the associated criteria might be ranked according to their importance. By ranking the criteria, one can specify a certain percentage for each criterion to express its importance in measurable terms. The associated percentage is referred to as the weight of the criterion in question, which shows how a certain criterion could influence the outcome of evaluating potential external contributors. For example, the weight of references regarding successfully completed similar projects is, say, 30%. This arrangement also makes it possible to interpret those differences between potential contributors that are qualitative by nature.

However, potential external contributors are different when measured against the different criteria (e.g., they might have a very different number of references). So the client organization needs to make two interrelated decisions on the following questions:

- What is the minimum acceptable level of capability for each criterion?
- What is the level of capability that is associated with the predefined weight for each criterion as the available maximum?

Let us consider the previous example again. One reference is the minimum requirement from the point of view of the related capability, while six references are considered to be quite enough in order to say that a potential contributor is absolutely capable from the point of view of the same criterion. This means that those potential external contributors who have six or more references regarding successfully completed similar projects are given 30% of the total number of scoring points. Based on these two extremes (the required minimum and the available maximum) that need to be defined for each criterion, one may develop a (nominal) scale by means of which the potential contributors could be evaluated. We need to bear in mind that depending on the applied project implementation strategy in the narrow sense, the minimum acceptable level of capability for certain criteria could be weighted even by zero. Based on the previous example it means that no reference is also accepted; however, in such a case, zero percent of the total scoring points is given.

By adopting the above idea (i.e., defining both the lowest and highest acceptable level of capability for each criterion) a client organization might ensure that:

- The relative importance of the criteria is maintained; however, the potential for maintaining the relative importance of the criteria heavily relies on the difference between the lowest and the highest acceptable and possible values. The bigger this difference for a given criterion, the lower the potential for maintaining the relative importance of the criterion in question. Clients, bearing in mind the implications of the applied project implementation strategy, need to make well-considered decisions in this respect.
- By specifying the lowest acceptable level of capability for each criterion, the client organizations make clear in advance the minimum level of capability that is required for qualification. Again, depending on the project implementation strategy in the narrow sense, the required minimum level of capability might be scored by zero percent for certain criteria.
- By specifying the acceptable lowest level capability for each criterion, instead of defining the total number of scoring points that needs to be achieved, the client organizations could avoid qualifying such potential contributors who show incapability against one or two criteria, while those who are good enough against the other criteria can achieve the total number of scores.
- Considering both the lowest and highest acceptable level of capability for each criterion, the client can develop a scale (generally a nominal scale) by means of which the applicants—the potential external contributors—might be reliably evaluated and qualified. The lower end of the scale represents the required lowest scores, while the high end of the scale represents the highest possible scores.

After developing an appropriate scale for each criterion involved for prequalification, the client can evaluate each applicant against each scale (i.e., each criterion). Those potential contributors who have met at least the minimum requirement for each criterion are considered to be qualified potential contributors. However, it is common that clients specify a percentage of the total scoring points as a certain kind of safety measurement which is higher than the sum of the lowest score-related percentages. This means that those potential contributors who want to be qualified need to satisfy a double-stage requirement. They need to satisfy the requirements of the lowest level capability for each criterion, as well as meeting the requirement of the previously mentioned minimum total scoring points.

Chapter 14

Project Implementation Strategy in the Broader Sense— Matching Tendering and Prequalification with Project Implementation Strategy

Previous chapters introduced the toolkit of project implementation strategy in the narrow sense, and also the toolkit for tendering and prequalification. It was also highlighted that in several cases prequalification is associated with tendering. At the same time, attention was paid to the potential impact of the project implementation strategy in the narrow sense on both prequalification and tendering. This chapter will highlight further this impact and the associated inter-relationships based on the author's research (Görög 2007) into project implementation strategy, and also based on experience gained from consultancy in project implementation strategy.

While both types of contracts and both types of payment can determine the use of prequalification, the use of tendering is affected by the types of contract in the first place. While various types of contracts and types of payment can be combined, the types of contracts naturally attract certain types of tendering. Bearing in mind these relationships, we also need to match tendering and prequalification with the predefined project implementation strategy in the narrow sense when we are concerned with developing project implementation strategy in the broader sense in the case of an external project.

This chapter highlights the fact that the matching of both prequalification and tendering for a predefined project implementation strategy in the narrow sense relies on the characteristics of the aforementioned types of contract, payment, tendering, and prequalification.

Matching Prequalification with Project Implementation Strategy

Previous chapters pointed out that different types of contract require a different level of project management professionalism in the client organization. It implies, at the same time, that these types of contracts also require different project management capability in the contributor organization. In other words, managing the implementation process of an external project needs to be shared among the client and the external contributors. The extent to which managing the implementation process is shifted onto the external contributors is determined by the contract type used. Thus, the client needs to have an external contributor who possesses the required project management capability. Consequently, in the course of prequalification, a client needs to find potential external contributors who possess project management capabilities that are suited to the project management task implicit in the type of contract used.

The type of contract selected for implementing an external project also determines the required technical capability of the external contributors, especially in terms of the scope of capability. The greater the number of work packages, the less the complexity of each package, while, of course, the fewer the work packages, the higher the complexity of each package; consequently, in the course of prequalification, a client should look for potential external contributors who possess technical capability that is in accordance with the complexity of the work package in question.

Both the type of payment and type of contract selected to implement an external project determine the required financial capability of the external contributors. However, these two different kinds of tool affect it basically in the same way. The price-based type of payment (either lump-sum price or unit prices/rates), due to its nature, shifts the risk associated with the implementation cost of the project work onto the external contributor. However, the smaller a work package is (because of the type of contract), the smaller the total contributor cost at risk. On the contrary, in big and complex project work, the contributor cost at risk is also higher. When using a cost-based type of payment—also due to its nature—the majority of those risks that are associated with the implementation cost are shifted onto the client. Consequently, the minority of those risks are borne by the contributor, and it is also appropriate that smaller work packages (because of the type of contract) lower the additional cost related risk borne by the contributor. Thus, a client organization needs to look for an external contributor in the course of prequalification with financial capability that is in accordance with the cost-related risk shifted upon and borne by the contributor.

Bearing in mind the interrelationships highlighted above, *the impact of types of contract on prequalification* that should be considered in the course of matching prequalification with project implementation strategy in the narrow sense is as follows:

- The use of a traditional type of contract will lower the importance of project management capability in accordance with the growing number of work packages. In such a case, a certain external contributor is expected to manage the implementation of a certain work package only. Consequently, this aspect of capability will have a lower rank relative to the criteria belonging to other capability aspects. However, it may happen that the total scores devoted to project management capability are given only to one or two criteria belonging to the project management capability aspect. The latter situation could result in a relatively high weight of these criteria, although the weight of the capability aspect as a whole will not change.

  The use of a traditional type of contract, at the same time, will lower the importance, and the associated rank and weight of the financial capability to a certain extent. It is also true when a traditional type of contract is coupled with a price-based type of payment. This is because, as it was pointed out earlier, the use of work packages lowers the contributor cost at risk.

  However, the use of a traditional type of contract could increase the importance, and the associated rank and weight of the technical capability in accordance with the growing number of work packages. This is explained by the role of the contributors working under the conditions of a traditional type of contract. In such a situation, the most significant obligation of a certain contributor is to perform a certain work package according to the predefined technical specifications.

- The use of a turnkey type of contract will heighten the importance of project management capability. It is justified, in general, by the nature of this type of contract. However, the responsibilities and risks that are shifted onto the turnkey contractor have a significant role in this respect. Consequently, this aspect of capability will have a higher rank, which means that the criteria belonging to this capability aspect will also have a higher total weight relative to the criteria belonging to other capability aspects.

  The use of a turnkey type of contract, at the same time, will heighten the importance, and the associated rank and weight of financial capability to a certain extent, even if it is coupled with a cost-based type of payment. The turnkey contractor is responsible for all the works encompassed in the implementation phase of the project. In this way, the cost-related risk of this primary stakeholder is more considerable than that of a contributor who is completing a work package under the conditions of the same type of payment.

  The use of a turnkey type of contract will also heighten the importance and the associated rank and weight of technical capability in the course of prequalification. Again, the turnkey contractor is responsible for all the work that is encompassed within the implementation phase of the project; thus, this stakeholder should technically also be capable of coping with the technical complexity of the implementation process as a whole.

- The use of a management type of contract can mean two different scenarios. The first one is when the management contractor is involved in prequalifying those external contributors who are potentially going to implement different work packages. Since the management contractor acts instead of, and on behalf of the client, this primary stakeholder needs to bear in mind those considerations that are mentioned in connection with the use of a traditional type of contract. The other case is the case of the client when this primary stakeholder is going to prequalify potential management contractors. Now the focus will be on the latter case.

  The primary obligation of the management contractor is to provide project management services, while the work packages themselves are implemented by external contributors. Therefore, the management contractor does not have a direct stake in completing these work packages. However, this primary stakeholder needs to accept a so-called management responsibility and the associated risk. Thus, the use of a management type of contract will heighten the importance of project management capability. Consequently, this aspect of capability will have a higher rank, which implies that the criteria belonging to this capability aspect will also have a higher total weight relative to the criteria belonging to other capability aspects.

  The use of a management type of contract, at the same time, will lower, in general, the importance and the associated rank and weight of financial capability to a certain extent. It results from the role of the management contractor, whereby this stakeholder does not have a direct stake in implementing the work.

- The use of a management type of contract means a lower importance, rank and weight of the technical capability in general in the course of prequalification. However, some criteria belonging to this capability aspect could be important. A management contractor needs to be skilled and experienced in those technical-related issues which are needed to supervise the implementation process. Thus, contrary to the lower importance of technical capability, a few of the technical-related criteria might have a relatively high weight, although the total weight of this capability aspect as a whole will not change.

Bearing in mind the interrelationships highlighted earlier, *the impact of the types of payment on prequalification* that might be considered in the course of matching prequalification with the project implementation strategy in the narrow sense is as follows:

- The use of a price-based type of payment will heighten the importance of financial capability since this payment type shifts the cost related risk onto

Table 14.1 Matching prequalification with the project implementation strategy

The Impact of Project Implementation Strategy	The Importance of Capability Aspects		
	Technical	Financial	Project Management

Types of contract
   Traditional
   Turnkey
   Management
	
	Higher
	Higher
	Lower
		
		Lower
		Higher
		Lower
			
			Lower
			Higher
			Higher

Types of payment
   Price-based
   Cost-based
   Target-based
		
		Higher
		Lower
		Moderate	

the external contributor. Consequently, this aspect of capability will have a higher rank, which implies that criteria belonging to this capability aspect will have a higher total weight in general relative to the criteria belonging to other capability aspects. However, a traditional type of contract, when it is coupled with a price-based type of payment, may moderate the importance of the financial capability. Contrary to a turnkey type of contract, the use of work packages lowers the contributor cost at risk.

- The use of a cost-based type of payment will, at the same time, lower the importance of the financial capability, since this payment type shifts the cost related risk onto the client organization. However, when a cost-based type of payment is coupled with a turnkey type of contract, because of the large scope of work, the importance of financial capability might be higher.
- Introducing target-based types of payment will generally moderate the importance of financial capability to a certain extent, since the use of target-based mechanisms results in a more balanced risk allocation in comparison with either the pure price-based or with the pure cost-based types of payment.

Table 14.1 conceptualizes the outcomes of the previously detailed matching of prequalification with project implementation strategy in the narrow sense.

Matching Tendering with Project Implementation Strategy

To reiterate, tendering is competitive bidding to select one or more external contributors to implement the project work. There are a few types of tendering, and a couple of them include prequalification as well. Thus, a client organization has the potential for selecting and applying the most appropriate. In the case of an external project, the client needs to use a type of tendering which ensures selecting reliable external contributors at the most economic cost. However, the type of tendering used should not restrict competition unreasonably. These requirements mean that there is a reasonable need to match tendering with the predefined project implementation strategy in the narrow sense in a reasonable manner. According to the author's research (Görög 2007), the contract type identified as part of the project implementation strategy plays a decisive role in the course of selecting the most appropriate type of tendering. Moreover, the type of contract in use naturally attracts the appropriate type of tendering.

Bearing in mind the requirements regarding the appropriateness of tendering, and the decisive role of the contract type in selecting the appropriate tendering type, the following relationships are considered in the course of matching tendering with project implementation strategy in the narrow sense.

Traditional Type of Contract

The traditional type of contract in general matches well the open tender, especially when there are many work packages. In such a case, as was emphasized earlier, there is potential to formulate work packages, that (compared to the entire scope of project work) imply low complexity and low implementation cost. Consequently, there is no need for both time- and cost-consuming prequalification since the required relatively low-level contributor capability could be reliably evaluated in the course of evaluating and ranking the submitted tender bids. Thus, the use of the traditional contract, in general, naturally attracts an open tender. In such a case, the potential contributors—the bidders—are requested to submit capability-related information along with their bid.

However, the traditional type of contract may well match the two-stage tender as well. Two-stage tendering implies that unit prices/rates are coupled with prequalification. This type of tendering provides the potential for utilizing the lowest unit prices/rates. By considering the lowest unit prices/rates submitted by qualified potential external contributors, the client is able to formulate such work packages that result in the most economic project implementation. That is, the work packages may be formulated based on the lowest unit prices/rates principle. Thus, the use of the traditional contract may naturally attract the two-stage type of tender.

Turnkey Type of Contract

The use of a turnkey type of contract requires prequalification for two reasons at least. One of the reasons is the responsibility and risk shifted onto the turnkey contractor. However, this primary stakeholder alone needs to take and bear all those responsibilities and risks that are associated with the entire project result and the whole duration time. Another reason is that a turnkey contract always limits the client's potential for exercising control over the implementation process. Under these conditions, a client needs to rely on the turnkey contractor, whereas the turnkey contractor should be reliable. The reliability (i.e., the capability) of a potential turnkey contractor might be evaluated by means of a farsighted prequalification. Thus, the use of a turnkey contract, in general, naturally attracts a selective tender.

At the same time, the turnkey type of contract matches well to the two-step tender as well. Two-step tendering implies that a proposal regarding the technical solution of the desired project result (or the problem to be solved by means of a project result) is coupled with prequalification. The viability of this type of tendering is justified since the desired project results could be achieved in many different ways, that is by means of many different technical solutions. (A good case in point is a market penetration project.) For a variety of reasons (e.g., lack of expertise), the client does not want to define a certain technical solution for realizing the expected project result. Instead, the client wants to utilize the professional competence of the potential external contributors. Two-step tendering provides potential for utilizing contributor expertise in such a case. However, developing a proposal by the potential external contributors for the technical solution of the desired project result could not be considered under the conditions of a traditional type of contract. Thus, the use of the turnkey contract may naturally attract a two-step type of tender.

Furthermore, a turnkey type of contract matches well a direct invitation tender. The idea of a direct invitation tender relies on a unique and novel know-how possessed by only a few potential external contributors. Consequently, because of the lack of expertise, the client is not able to define adequately the expected project result and the associated project work. Since the client could not develop an appropriate project definition, there is no potential for reliably prequalifying potential external contributors. On the other hand, there is no potential for qualifying others except those with the know-how. Thus, the client invites these potential contributors to prepare and submit their bid. Thus, the use of a turnkey contract may naturally attract a direct-invitation tender.

Management Type of Contract

From the point of view of tendering, the use of a management type of contract, to a certain extent, resembles using a turnkey type of contract. Since the client entrusts managing the project implementation process to a management contractor who acts on behalf of the client, the management contractor also needs to be reliable. The reliability (i.e., the capability) of a potential management contractor might be evaluated by means of prequalification. Thus, the management type of contract naturally attracts a selective tender.

Table 14.2 conceptualizes the outcomes of the previously detailed matching of tendering with the types of contract.

Table 14.2 Matching tendering with the types of contract

Types of Contract	Types of Tendering Naturally Attracted
Traditional	Open tender
	Two-stage tender
Turnkey	Selective tender
	Two-step tender
	Direct invitation tender
Management	Selective tender

The use of a *serial tender* (when a client wants to implement the same project a few times but in different locations, for example, petrol stations; or when a client wants to implement a complex information system in a stage-by-stage manner) is generally a special case. The first part (or the first few parts) of the project (or program) could be awarded by means of open or selective or two-tier tendering, while the subsequent parts are negotiated based on invitation with those previous contributors with whom the client is satisfied.

Case Examples Demonstrating Matching

Real Estate Development Project

Chapter 12 outlined a project implementation strategy formulated by the client in the narrow sense, both in terms of types of contract and types of payment. This project implementation strategy tends to be based on traditional type of contract and price-based (lump-sum) type of payment. The following work packages were formulated: construction and installation design, civil engineering construction, and building engineering installation. The project client, taking into consideration the identified project implementation strategy, decided to apply selective tendering for each work package. The underlying reasoning for the client's decision is as follows.

A traditional type of contract is applied; however, each single work package seems to be complex because of the high complexity of the entire project. Construction and installation design work packages tend to be complex by nature and interrelated. They therefore need to be completed in accordance with the associated construction and installation drawings. That is why the work package of design has a significant role in this project implementation strategy. However, the other two work packages are also complex.

Taking into account the considerations regarding matching tendering with project implementation strategy in the narrow sense, the client made a wise decision when selective tendering was selected for each work package. As for matching prequalification with project implementation strategy, the three work packages— in spite of the natural differences due to the different scope of work—comprise many similarities. Thus, in the course of introducing prequalification, this project will concentrate only on the construction work package. According to the project implementation strategy (traditional type of contract and lump-sum price), the client organization ranked and weighted the three aspects of capability, and the associated criteria as follows:

- Technical capability: maximum 40%
- Financial capability: maximum 35%
- Project management capability: maximum 25%

As for the *technical capability*, the client considered all four previously out-lined criteria (see Chapter 13) to be important. They were ranked and weighted (bearing in mind the maximum 40% weight of this capability aspect) in the following way:

- References regarding successfully completed similar project works: 15% for five or more references (minimum weight: 3% for one reference)
- Resources available for the project works: 10%
  - Human resources: 4%, if all the predefined key technicians are employed by the applicant (minimum weight: 1%, if 50% of the predefined key technicians are employed by the applicant)
  - Plants: 6%, if all the predefined key equipment and machines are owned by the applicant (minimum weight: 2%, if 50% of the predefined key equipment and machines are owned by the applicant)
- Familiarity with, and experience in working in accordance with the required technical specifications: 8%, if all the predefined technical staff is employed by the applicant (minimum weight: 2%, if 50% of the predefined technical staff is employed by the applicant)
- Quality assurance regarding the project works: 7%, if externally audited quality assurance is in use in the applicant's organization (minimum weight: 0%, if only quality control is in use in the applicant's organization)

Regarding the *financial capability*, balance sheets of the previous three years, and also the profit-and-loss statements of the previous three years were considered (bearing in mind the maximum 35% weight of this capability aspect) in the following way:

- Profit and loss statements: 20%, if the average profit of the previous three years is not less than the estimated cost of the work package (minimum weight: 5%, if the average profit of the previous three years is not less than 50% of the estimated cost of the work package)
- Balance sheets: 15%, if the liabilities do not exceed 50% of the sources of capital (minimum weight: 5%, if the liabilities do not exceed 60% of the sources of capital)

Neither credibility nor financial liability insurance policy was considered by the client in the course of this prequalification. It was expected that based on the above two criteria, the financial suitability of the applicants (the potential contributors) could be reliably evaluated.

The *project management capability* of the potential external contributors was also evaluated by means of two criteria (bearing in mind the maximum 25% weight of this capability aspect) for the same reason that was mentioned in connection with the financial capability. The criteria and the associated weights are as follows:

- Project management expertise: 18%, if the predefined number of trained and experienced project management professionals are employed by the applicant (minimum weight: 2%, if 50% of the predefined number of trained and experienced project management practitioners are employed by the applicant)
- Project management quality assurance: 7%, if externally audited quality assurance is in use in the applicant's organization (minimum weight: 2% if there is only some internally elaborated policy in use in the applicant's organization)

The case introduced above illustrates, on the one hand, the impact of applied project implementation strategy in the narrow sense on the use of prequalification. It also illustrates, on the other hand, the right use of the scoring point system to qualify potential external contributors. By specifying minimum weight (as well as the maximum weight) for each criterion, the client can maintain the relative importance of the criteria in accordance with the requirements of the project implementation strategy in the narrow sense. The use of minimum weight, however, expresses the lowest acceptable capability level against the criteria, although the minimum weight could even be zero in the case of a certain criterion.

The introduction of both minimum and maximum weight at the same time makes it possible to develop, say, a nominal scale to compare, that is, to evaluate applicants reliably. The client in the above project, bearing in mind both minimum and maximum weights given in terms of percentage for each criterion considered, developed a nominal scale for each criterion to evaluate applicants in order to identify capable potential external contributors.

Information System Project

Chapter 12 introduced the project implementation strategy both in terms of type of contract and type of payment that was formulated by the project client with the help of independent consultants. The identified project implementation strategy in the narrow sense encompassed the use of a management type of contract and price-based (lump-sum) type of payment (in connection with the management contractor). The final decision regarding the work packages was made by the management contractor, and these packages were contracted out (on behalf of the client) based on the type of payment that was also decided by the management contractor.

The rest of this section will concentrate on the type of tendering used by the client to select a management contractor. Independent consultants were involved in making a decision on the type of tendering. The outcome of the decision-making process was to apply selective tendering, which implies the use of prequalification. The use of prequalification is absolutely justified when a management type of contract is used.

The management contractor is responsible for managing the implementation of the whole project, as this primary stakeholder acts on behalf of the client. It means that the client needs to rely on the management contractor, that is, the management contractor needs to be reliable or, in other words, adequately prequalified.

Accordingly, three aspects of capability and the associated criteria were ranked and weighted as follows:

- Project management capability: maximum 65%
- Technical capability: maximum 20%
- Financial capability: maximum 15%

The *project management capability* of the potential management contractors were evaluated by means of all the four criteria (bearing in mind the maximum 65% weight of this capability aspect) mentioned in Chapter 13. The criteria and the associated weights are as follows:

- Project management expertise: 20%, if the predefined number of trained and experienced project management professionals are employed by the applicant (minimum weight: 10%, if 75% of the predefined number of trained and experienced project management professionals are employed by the applicant)
- Project management quality assurance: 15%, if externally audited quality assurance is in use in the applicant's organization (minimum weight: 5%, if only internally sanctioned quality assurance is in use in the applicant's organization)
- References that testify the applicant successfully completed projects as management contractor: 15%, if five or more references (minimum weight: 6%, if two references)
- Organizational arrangement at project level: 15%, if the predefined management team is deployed solely to the project (minimum weight: 5%, if only the project manager is deployed solely to the project)

The organizational arrangement at company level and the reporting relationship between the two management levels was considered to be important when using a turnkey type of contract. Thus, this issue was not considered as capability criterion.

In connection with the *technical capability* of the potential management contractors, two criteria (bearing in mind the maximum 20% weight of this capability aspect) were used to qualify them. The criteria and the associated weights are as follows:

- References regarding successfully completed similar project work: 15%, if five or more references (minimum weight: 3%, if one reference)
- Quality assurance regarding the project work: 5%, if externally audited quality assurance is in use in the applicant's organization (minimum weight: 2% if only an internally developed policy is in use in the applicant's organization)

Regarding the *financial capability*, only the profit and loss statements of the previous three years were considered (bearing in mind the maximum 15% weight of this capability aspect) in the following way:

- Profit and loss statements: 15%, if the average profit of the previous three years is not less than 50% of the estimated cost of the entire project (minimum weight: 5%, if the average profit of the previous three years is not less than 25% of the estimated cost of the entire project)

The use of a management type of contract and the associated role of the management contractor explain the importance of the capability aspects considered in this project. Although the weight of the financial capability seems to be low, we need to bear in mind that a management contractor generally does not have that much money directly at stake.

The previously introduced issue of prequalification also illustrates how an applied project implementation strategy in the narrow sense affects the use of criteria. It also illustrates how to ensure a firm basis for developing appropriate evaluation scales. By means of specifying minimum weight (as well as the maximum weight) for each criterion, the client can ensure the relative importance of the criteria in accordance with the requirements of the project implementation strategy. The use of minimum weights, however, expresses the lowest acceptable capability level against the criteria.

At the same time, the above case also illustrates how a certain type of contract naturally attracts a certain type of tendering.

Chapter 15

Bid Evaluation—Ranking the Tender Bids

Bid evaluation (also referred to as bid assessment, tender analysis, tender appraisal, or proposal evaluation) is a step in the process of formulating and executing project implementation strategy. One of the submitted bids (also referred to as offers, tenders, or proposals) is found to be the best bid, and the bidder (also referred to as tenderer) of the best bid is chosen to be external contributor. If the so-called best bid is accepted within the predefined validity term, a contractual relationship is agreed between the client and the bidder, that is, the contributor. Thus, identifying and accepting the best bid needs to be a very well-considered task in the client organization. This chapter is going to provide an introduction to the aim of bid evaluation, and a special attention will be paid to ranking the submitted bids. Multi-criteria based bid ranking technique will be emphasized, while highlighting the impact of the applied project implementation strategy in the narrow sense, and its interrelationships with tendering and the associated prequalification.

The Aim of Bid Evaluation

In order to consider properly the aim of bid evaluation, we first need to consider the aim of the bid itself, and the aim of the underlying bid invitation (also referred to as tender documentation). Let us start with the last phenomenon.

One of the most important aims of a bid invitation is to define the project work to be implemented, either in terms of the tasks belonging to a work-package to be completed (e.g., when using a traditional type of contract) or in terms of the desired project result (e.g., when using a turnkey type of contract). The other fundamental aim is to define those conditions under which the project works are to be implemented. These conditions need to include not only the technical conditions (e.g., standards, specifications, etc.) but the financial conditions (e.g., terms of payment) and the legal conditions (e.g., third-party liability) or any other important conditions (e.g., validity period of the bids, completion date, etc.). Finally, the third fundamental aim of a bid invitation is to define the testing of the completed project work which might be especially important when using a turnkey type of contract. In case of the latter, the testing of the entire completed project result needs to be defined in a very precise manner. However, defining the tests also could include technical, financial, legal, and other conditions and consequences that are related to the tests.

By satisfying the requirements in the above-mentioned fundamental aims, a bid invitation provides a firm basis for developing bids. In this way, project work and the associated conditions of implementation, as well as the conditions of testing, can be considered by the potential external contributors as well (i.e., they rely on the same information base). This latter potential, from the point of view of the client organizations, has the following advantages:

- Due to the predefined conditions, there is a potential for clear competition.
- Since each submitted bid should be based on the same set of conditions (a common information base), bids are comparable (i.e., there is potential for objective bid ranking).
- The previous two conditions make it possible to identify the best bid (i.e., the bid that offers the most economic implementation of the project work or the entire project result). The most economic project implementation is not necessarily the cheapest project implementation.

Bidding is undertaken by the potential external contributors (here they are referred to as bidders) in response to an invitation issued by the client. The ultimate aim of a bid is to demonstrate the readiness of the chosen bidder to enter into a contractual relationship with the client and for completing the associated contractual obligations. However, from the point of view of the bidders, the other important aim of a bid is to provide protection for the bidder since upon accepting the bid as it stands, a contractual relationship formally begins between the client and the bidder. That is, when the client informs the bidder that the bid is accepted, both the parties are legally bound. Further discussion of this latter aim of a bid is beyond the scope of this book.

Bearing in mind the above considerations, we could say that the ultimate aim of bid evaluation is ensuring proper project implementation at the most economical cost. This final aim of the bid evaluation satisfies both the final aims of a bid invitation and of the bids themselves that are developed and submitted based on the bid invitation.

Satisfying the final aim of the bid evaluation, at the same time, requires two kinds of evaluations, such as preliminary examination and bid ranking.

The primary purpose of the *preliminary examination* is identifying eligible bids by means of addressing the question whether the submitted bids are in compliance with the underlying bid invitation in terms of:

- The scope of the project work;
- The conditions of implementing the project work;
- The conditions of testing the completed project work or the project result itself;

- The other conditions specified in the bid invitation; and
- Completeness of the attachments.

The preliminary examination, however, may include checking and correcting arithmetical errors when unit prices/rates are in use as payment type (errors in multiplying unit prices/rates by the associated quantity, and errors in totaling the previous outcomes). A bid is considered to be eligible if it is found to be in compliance with the conditions and other requirements specified in the bid invitation.

Bid ranking focuses on ranking those bids that are found to be eligible in course of the preliminary examination in order to identify the best bid. Bearing in mind the final aim of bid evaluation (i.e., ensuring proper project implementation at the most economical cost), one can understand that the cheapest bid is not necessarily the best bid.

Existing literature on bid evaluation, including both the earlier and the more recent literature generally does not differentiate clearly between the preliminary examination of bids and the ranking of bids. However, authors (e.g., Bower, in Bower 2003c; Gido and Clements 1999; Schwalbe 2004; Bower and Smith, in Smith 1995) emphasize the need for matching submitted bids to the conditions of bid invitations. However, this matching, according to most of the previously cited authors generally belongs to a pre-selection process aimed at identifying the most attractive bids. Another characteristic of the existing literature on bid evaluation is failing to consider the type of tender and the project implementation strategy in the narrow sense. It is suggested in this literature to consider the typical prequalification criteria as bid evaluation (ranking) criteria. Bower and Smith (in Smith 1995) may be the only exception to this statement who defined the aim of bid evaluation with regard to payment types. However, they did not define the associated evaluation criteria. Watt, Kayis, and Willey (2009, 2010) highlight in their research that selecting bid ranking criteria is generally based on a certain kind of organizational usage, while subjectivity is also experienced.

Essentially, the approach toward bid evaluation in the existing literature implies that bid evaluation, and especially ranking the bids to identify the best bid, is basically an independent task with no regard for the potential interrelationships with its wider context. However, neglecting these interrelationships could limit those advantages of tendering that were pointed out earlier in this chapter. Consequently, the traditional approach could lead to identifying a bid as the best bid, which results in project implementation that will not fully support the long-term interest of the client organization. The following part of this chapter, among other issues, highlights those factors that may have an impact on identifying the appropriate ranking criteria.

Ranking the Bids

There are a few possible tools by means of which eligible bids might be ranked; however, this book considers only the two most widely used bid ranking techniques. These are the life cycle cost principle and the merit point system.

It is worth noting that life cycle cost might also be considered as one of the criteria in the course of using the merit point system.

Bid Ranking by Means of the Life Cycle Cost Principle

Life cycle cost associated with a project result is the sum of the acquisition cost (the total project implementation cost, for example, the contract price), plus the so-called follow-on ownership cost incurred in the initial phase of the operational life cycle of the completed project result. Because of the time-value of money, the follow-on ownership cost should be discounted to present value (PV) by means of the appropriate discount factors. However, the acquisition cost of the project result is considered to be the same as present value.

Ranking the submitted bids by means of the life cycle cost principle means that there may be a difference not only between the bid price of two or more competing bids, but also with the follow-on ownership cost associated with the project results as well. The follow-on ownership cost might generally be different due to the different technical solutions offered by different bidders to bring about the same project outcome. The potential for utilizing the likely advantages of the different technical solutions of the same project outcome might be considered only when a turnkey type of contract is used. The client also needs to be aware of the acquisition cost (the total project implementation cost) in advance, which is not the case when a cost-based type of payment is in use. Both considerations mean that ranking the submitted bids by using the life cycle cost principle can be done when the client applies a turnkey type of contract and lump-sum price as project implementation strategy in the narrow sense. However, the use of the life cycle principle also presumes that the client is adopting a long-term perspective.

In terms of the follow-on ownership cost during the initial phase of the operational life cycle of the completed project outcome, the main costs items are as follows:

- Maintenance cost
- Operational cost
- Upgrading/modernizing cost
- Estimated residual scrap value (when appropriate)

Furthermore, the life cycle cost principle may also be utilized to evaluate the impact of different technical solutions of the project outcome in terms of:

- Productivity (total life cycle cost/unit of output)
- Efficiency (difference in terms of total life cycle cost)

When the life cycle cost principle is in use to rank bids, it is quite obvious that the best bid is the one which results in the lowest life cycle cost.

Table 15.1 Comparing two bids (efficiency)

Cost-Related Items	Bid A	Bid B
	(Values in Thousands)	
Bid Price	(+) 130.000	(+) 141.000
Operational Cost (10 years)	65.000	58.000
Maintenance Cost (10 years)	20.000	16.000
PV of the Operational Cost (12%)	(+) 36,731.5	(+) 32,775.8
PV of the Maintenance Cost (12%)	(+) 11.302	(+) 9,041.6
Cost Saving due to Higher Efficiency	–	15.000
PV of the Cost Saving (12%)	–	(-) 8,476.5
Total Life Cycle Cost	178,033.5	174,340.9
Ranking	2	1

The following two tables illustrate the use of the life cycle principle. Table 15.1 shows a comparison of two competing bids that offered different boilers for a straw-fired power plant project.

Table15.2 also compares two competing bids; however, in this example the bidders offered different technical solutions in terms of productivity for a fertilizer plant.

It is interesting to note that people often instinctively rely on the life cycle principle. Good cases in point are buying a new car, buying household equipment, and so forth.

Bid Ranking by Means of the Merit Point System

Ranking the submitted bids using a merit point system, from the point of view of the evaluation technique, resembles the scoring point system used in prequalification. However, both the aim of evaluation and the criteria are different. The aim here is,

Table 15.2 Comparing two bids (productivity)

Cost-Related Items	Bid A	Bid B
	(Values in Thousands)	
Bid Price	(+) 1.200	(+) 1.500
Operational Cost (5 years)	500	550
Maintenance Cost (5 years)	100	110
PV of the Operational Cost (12%)	(+) 360.5	(+) 396.6
PV of the Maintenance Cost (12%)	(+) 72.1	(+) 79.3
Total Life Cycle Cost	1,632.6	1,975.9
Output per Year	120.000 tons	150.000 tons
Life Cycle Cost per ton of Output	2.721	2,634.5
Ranking	2	1

similar to the life cycle cost principle, identifying the best eligible bid. To achieve this end we need to go through the following steps:

- Identifying criteria to rank the bids
- Determining the relative importance of each criterion
- Ranking the criteria based on their importance, and weighting them based on their rank
- Developing a ranking scale for each criterion
- Matching each bid against each criterion by means of the ranking scale
- Identifying the best bid

Factors that Determine the Potential Ranking Criteria

The author's previous research and experiences gained from consultancy suggest that there are factors that greatly determine the potential ranking criteria, such as:

- Type of tendering used in the course of selecting external contributors.
- Completeness of the bid invitation in terms of conditions of implementing the project work.
- The client's interest in gaining better achievement in terms of:
  - Technical parameters (e.g., energy consumption, the required operational staff, better operational quality, etc.),
  - Standardization of the built-in parts encompassed by the project result.
- Other potential requirements of the client, such as:
  - Availability of maintenance service during the operational phase,
  - Possibility for upgrading/modernizing, and for capacity enlargement,
  - Length of the guarantee period.
- The life cycle cost associated with the bids.
- Bid price or fee (when using a cost-based type of payment).

Type of tendering could either increase or decrease the number of likely ranking criteria. When a tender type in use requires prequalification, there is no need to consider prequalification criteria as ranking criteria since only qualified potential contributors have the opportunity to submit their bid. Contrary to the previous case, when the type of tender in use did not require prequalification, it seems wise to include a few prequalification criteria too (i.e., the most decisive ones in the given context) when ranking the bids together with other ranking criteria.

Completeness of the bid invitation implies that a client deliberately does not specify a certain condition of the implementation (e.g., completion date, terms of payment, etc.) in order to use it as a ranking criterion along with other ranking criteria.

The client's interest in gaining a better outcome than specified may be a reasonable ranking criterion. For example, the lower the likely energy consumption and the number of staff members needed to operate the project result, the lower the likely total operational cost associated with the completed project outcome will be.

However, the higher the number of standard built-in parts of the project outcome, the lower the likely future maintenance cost incurred during the operational phase of the completed project outcome will be.

Other potential requirements of the client, similar to the client's interest in gaining a better outcome than specified, may relate to the follow-on ownership cost associated with the completed project result. If a bidder, when requested by the client, offers reliable service potential during the operational phase of the project result or a longer guarantee period, etc. the client may have lower future maintenance costs. At the same time, other potential elements, such as capacity enlargement, may enable the client organization to maximize future business opportunities.

The life cycle cost associated with bids might also be considered as one of the ranking criteria. However, both the client's interest in gaining a better outcome than specified and the other potential requirements of the client mentioned previously are life cycle cost-related considerations to a certain extent. However, if total life cycle cost is considered as one ranking criterion amongst other required criteria in a given case, this might provide the potential for a more complex multidimensional bid-ranking approach. This is especially true when the potential differences between the follow-on operational costs are significant.

Bid price or the fee is often the most important ranking criterion, and needs to be a major consideration of the client when ranking the eligible bids.

Figure 15.1 visualizes the relationship between the likely number of the ranking criteria and the determining factors.

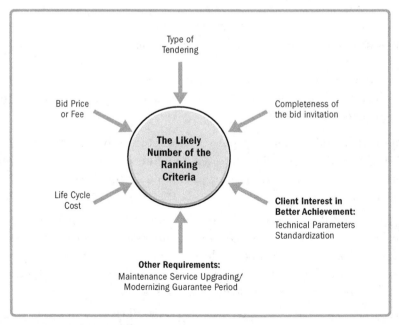

Figure 15.1 Factors determining the number of ranking criteria

Identifying Criteria to Rank the Bids and Determining their Relative Importance

When a client organization is identifying ranking criteria for a particular case, there is a need to consider those factors that may determine the potential ranking criteria. The impacts of the type of tendering are clear and self-evident, as it was discussed in the previous part of this chapter. It is also beyond a doubt that bid price or the fee (when using a cost-based type of payment) needs to be considered as a ranking criterion in the course of identifying the best bid. As for inclusion of other potential ranking criteria, the client needs to formulate a definite answer to the following questions:

1. Is there any clear advantage to leaving one (or more) conditions of implementing the project open?
2. Is there any clear advantage to achieving a better-than-specified outcome by means of specific technical parameters or standardization?
3. Is there any clear advantage to including maintenance service provided by the external contributor, a longer guarantee period, the possibility to upgrade/modernize, or some other supply element offered by the bidders?
4. Are there any significant differences between the follow-on ownership costs as a result of the different technical solutions offered by the bidders?

When the answer to a certain question is a definite yes, the associated criterion might reasonably be included as a ranking criterion. When the ranking criteria have been identified, the client needs to define their importance relative to each other. To this end, the client might take into account:

- The underlying strategic objective of the project
- The additional future potential that may be derived from the better than specified project result
- The potential future follow-on cost associated with the project outcome
- The maximum amount of money the client has for implementing the desired project outcome

The above considerations may have interrelated impacts on the importance of the potential bid-ranking criteria. However, the author will not highlight all the possible impacts; instead, the focus is on those impacts that are considered to be the most important by the author.

The underlying strategic objective of the project may shape the importance of those criteria included that are related to the duration time of implementation (e.g., completion date). Thus, if the time scale is urgent, the bid price (or the fee) might have a lower importance. However, the use of a time target in the type of payment may exclude the issue of urgency in the ranking system.

The additional future potential that may be derived from the project result should necessitate considering the possibility for upgrading/modernizing, or the capacity enlargement itself as an important ranking criterion. The price related criterion again might have a relatively lower importance in this case.

The potential future follow-on cost associated with the project outcome may result in the greater importance of the technical parameters mentioned earlier in this chapter, and that of standardization, and maintenance service provided by the contributor, and the length of the guarantee period. The total future follow-on cost associated with the project result could vary according to technical solutions offered by the bidders, however, and it may necessitate including life cycle cost as a bid ranking criterion. The importance of the life cycle cost as a bid ranking criterion might be relatively high, while again, the importance of the price-related criterion may be relatively low.

The maximum amount of money that could be devoted to implementing the desired project result may have a considerable impact on the importance of the price-related criteria. When there is no flexibility regarding the predefined amount of money or the money devoted to project implementation is considered to be a scarce resource, price-related ranking criteria might have a great importance.

Table 15.3 summarizes the relationships between the above four factors and the relative importance of the related bid ranking criteria.

Table 15.3 Impact of the factors determining the relative importance of the ranking criteria

Factors	The Concerned Criterion	Impact	
		In Case of Urgency	**No Urgency**
Underlying strategic objective	Time-related criterion (e.g., completion date)	Higher importance	Lower importance
	Price-related criterion (e.g., bid price)	Lower importance	Higher importance
		Prosperous Potential	**No Potential**
Future potential	Upgrading/modernizing	Higher importance	Lower importance
	Capacity enlargement	Higher importance	Lower importance
	Price-related criterion (e.g., bid price)	Lower importance	Higher importance
Follow-on cost	Technical parameters	Higher importance	
	Standardization	Higher importance	
	Maintenance service	Higher importance	
	Guarantee period	Higher importance	
	Price-related criterion (e.g., bid price)	Lower importance	
		Flexible	**Fixed**
Amount of money devoted to the project	Price-related criterion (e.g., bid price)	Lower importance	Higher importance

Developing a Ranking Scale for Each Criterion

After determining the relative importance of each criterion that is included in ranking the bids, the criteria themselves should be ranked based on their importance. Then, based on their individual rank, the criteria need to be weighted in order to make an evaluation scale for each criterion. The weight of each criterion shows, in terms of percentage, the extent to which it has an impact on ranking the bids. The use of ranking scales enables the client organization to score the bids. Depending on the criterion in question, a given scale could be either progressive or regressive by nature. However, in both cases there is a need for a base value from which the scale itself can be developed. This base value could even be zero, typically when a progressive scale is in use.

As for the *regressive scale*, typical cases in point are the use of bid price and life cycle cost as ranking criteria. Let us consider the following example. The bid price (lump-sum), due to its importance for the client, has a 60% weight. This is considered to be the base value of the scale associated with the bid price, and, at the same time, it is considered to be the maximum value that could be associated with the bid price. Thus, the lowest price bid is given 60% of the total number of merit points. The client decided to use a scale in which a 1% price difference in comparison with the lowest bid price will result in 1% deduction from the merit points that are given to the best price bid. When a regressive scale is in use, the maximum value of each scale is determined by the maximum weight of the chosen criterion.

A *progressive scale* generally implies a zero base value, since this type of scale is normally used for ranking criteria when the client determines a definite minimum expectation (e.g., the length of the guarantee period). However, bidders have the potential to offer some more advantageous possibilities. Those bidders who meet the client's minimum expectation are given zero merit points, while those who offer a better possibility (e.g., a longer guarantee period) are given more merit points accordingly. This kind of progressive scale may also be used when the client does not determine any expectation in connection with a certain criterion (e.g., maintenance service during the operational phase), but the bidders have the potential to include it in their offer. When a progressive scale is in use, there is a need to define a maximum value that expresses the maximum weight of the criterion in question. Thus, the maximum value expresses the importance of each criterion. Otherwise, the relative importance of the criteria in question might be invalidated due to the potentially significant differences of the related offers.

From the point of view of practicability, it is wise to maximize the number of total merit points to 100. It enables client organizations to interpret percentages in numerical terms easily (i.e., number of merit points). Taking into account the implications of both the progressive and the regressive scales in connection with the previous maximum value, the total sum of the maximum values associated either with the progressive or with the regressive scales needs to be 100.

Identifying the Best Bid

In order to identify the best bid, the client first needs to match each bid against each criterion by means of the previously developed ranking scales. The matching results in merit points that are given to each bid against each criterion. Then, the given merit points are added up to determine the total number of merit points gained by each bid. The bid that has gained the highest number of merit points is considered to be the best bid.

Case Examples for Bid Ranking

Real Estate Development Project

Chapter 12 introduced the project implementation strategy in the narrow sense applied in this project (traditional type of contract and price-based—lump-sum—type of payment), and Chapter 14 discussed the use of selective tendering to find the external contributors who will implement the project work. As in the introduction of prequalification in Chapter 14, in the course of introducing bid ranking used by the client in this project, we focus on the construction work-package again. First let us see the impact of those factors that determine the potential ranking criteria.

Type of tendering (the selective tendering) used by the client for selecting construction contributor required prequalification. Thus, there was no need for considering prequalification criteria in the course of ranking the bids since only qualified potential contributors submitted their bid. The bid invitation was considered to be complete in terms of each different kind of condition with regards to implementing the project and to performing tests. Although the desired project result was defined and fixed clearly in a very detailed manner, the client was interested neither in achieving a better outcome in terms of different technical parameters or in heightening the level of standardization of the built-in parts. As for the other potential requirements, the client showed interest in a guarantee period that was longer than was stipulated by law. Because of the clear and detailed project scope definition, there was no potential for significant differences between the follow-on ownership costs, while the bid price (i.e., the cost of the project implementation) was an important issue in the client organization.

Taking into account the four questions outlined in the previous part of this chapter, one could say that the client might give a definite yes only in the case of the third question because of the expected advantage gained by the potentially longer guarantee period. Consequently, the client justifiably uses two ranking criteria, namely the *bid price* and the *length of the guarantee period*. Taking into account those considerations that may have an impact on defining the importance of the ranking criteria (see previous part of this chapter) the amount of money that might be devoted to implementing the desired project result is found to be a significant factor. The client decided to use a progressive scale to rank the bids from the point of view of the offered

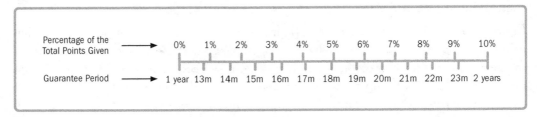

Figure 15.2 Ranking scale for the guarantee period

guarantee period, while a regressive scale was used to rank the bids based on the bid price. Figure 15.2 and Figure 15.3, respectively, show the associated scales.

Based on the relative importance of the guarantee period. 10% was defined as a maximum value, while the base value because of the progressive scale used in this case was zero. Each additional month regarding the length of the offered guarantee period will increase the number of merit points given to the bidder by 0.833 percent. The bidder offering a guarantee period over two years will be given the maximum number of merit points (i.e., 10%).

Bearing in mind the importance of the involved criteria, the determined weight of the bid price was 90%, which was considered to be the base value of the scale, and also the maximum value that could be associated with the bid price. Each half a percent difference in comparison with the lowest price bid will deduct the number of merit points given to the bidder by 0.5 percent.

The client of this project ranked five eligible bids. Due to the nature of this project (low level of uncertainty), there were no significant differences regarding the bid prices; however, offers regarding the length of the guarantee period varied considerably. It explains why the third-lowest price bid was considered to be the best bid, while a regressive scale was used to rank the bids based on the bid price.

Information System Project

Chapter 12 also introduced the project implementation strategy in the narrow sense for the information system project, where a management type of contract and a price-based (lump-sum) type of payment were applied. Chapter 14 then outlined the use of

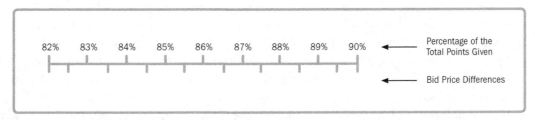

Figure 15.3 Ranking scale for the bid price

selective tendering to find an appropriate management contractor who would manage the implementation of the project. Here, bid-ranking is considered for this project. However, because of the use of a management contract and the associated role of the management contractor, ranking the bids submitted by the potential contractors is not a very complex process. Nevertheless, let us see the role of those factors that determine the potential ranking criteria in this case.

The selective tendering used by the client for selecting a management contractor required a form of prequalification that did not necessitate considering prequalification criteria in the course of ranking the bids, since only qualified potential management contractors submitted their bids. The bid invitation was considered to be complete in terms of the conditions. The role of the management contractor was defined and fixed clearly in a very detailed manner. The client's potential interest in achieving a better than specified outcome (in terms of technical parameters and standardization) could not be interpreted in connection with the role of the management contractor. The other potential requirements of the client (outlined in the previous parts of this chapter) also could not be interpreted when the role of a management contractor is considered. However, the bid price was the only important issue in the client organization.

Taking into consideration the four questions and the associated considerations outlined in the previous section of this chapter, one could say that the client justifiably uses only one ranking criteria (i.e., the *bid price* specified by the bidders).

The use of bid price as the single bid-ranking criterion is nevertheless supported by relatively strict evaluation scales that were used in the course of prequalifying potential management contractors. There was a relatively narrow range between the maximum and the minimum weights for each prequalification criterion; however, there was no zero minimum weight in use.

The client of the ERP project ranked three eligible bids, and a regressive scale was used to rank them. In spite of the precisely formulated bid invitation, there were significant differences amongst the bid prices. It explains why the lowest price bid was found to be the best bid. This case example demonstrates how the tools of project implementation strategy in the broader sense are interrelated in the course of their use.

Chapter 16

Implications for Clients and External Contributors

The first chapters introduced how the concept of project implementation strategy for external projects is considered in this book. The subsequent chapters discussed the toolkit of project implementation strategy as well as the appropriate use of this toolkit. At the same time, the interrelationships between the tools within the toolkit of project implementation strategy in the broader sense were also highlighted.

First, the project implementation strategy in the narrow sense (i.e., the type of contract and the type of payment) needs to be formulated. The outcome of making decisions on the project implementation strategy in the narrow sense determines the use of tendering, as well as the occasionally associated prequalification. In other words, tendering and prequalification need to be matched with the project implementation strategy in the narrow sense. Ranking the submitted tender bids is also determined directly or indirectly by both the project implementation strategy in the narrow sense and the type of tendering used, as well as by the use of prequalification.

In other words, the previous chapters focused on the appropriate use of the tools of project implementation strategy in an external project context, including the interrelationships between these tools. Here, in the last chapter, the author focuses on highlighting the advantages that may be gained when the client in an external project devises an effective project implementation strategy.

Implications for Clients

The client organization is the main stakeholder that initiates a project. This stakeholder should, therefore, not delegate making decisions on the project implementation strategy to others in an external project. Thus, it seems to be justified to start highlighting the potential advantages of an appropriately designed project implementation strategy from the point of view of the client organization.

- A project implementation strategy in the narrow sense implies the type of payment and the type of contract. This project implementation strategy is considered to be appropriate if:
  - An applied type of contract makes the project implementation process and the associated project management more efficient.
  - An applied type of contract makes it possible for the client to test and prove reliably the completed project result.
  - An applied type of payment makes the cost related risks born by the parties manageable.
  - An applied type of payment makes it possible for the client to achieve a better outcome than specified if it is reasonable.

In brief, a project implementation strategy in the narrow sense is appropriate if the responsibilities and risks (associated with the project triangle) are allocated in line with both the client and the project characteristics. Chapter 12 introduced the approach by means of which a project implementation strategy in the narrow sense meets the above requirements can be formulated for an external project. When a project implementation strategy in the narrow sense is considered to be appropriate, it contributes to the success of the project. Such a project implementation strategy contributes to achieving success not only in terms of the project triangle but also in terms of the client satisfaction, since it makes managing changes easier in the course of implementing the project. At the same time, success achieved against these two criteria may foster stakeholder acceptance (i.e., stakeholder satisfaction), which is also a very important success criterion.

- Based on the outcome of formulating the appropriate project implementation strategy in the narrow sense, especially based on the identified type of contract, the client can identify the most appropriate type of tender. Chapter 14 outlined how certain types of contract naturally attract certain types of tenders. Since prequalification is both time consuming and costly, prequalification should only be used when it is justified. There is also potential for applying prequalification in accordance with the requirements of the project implementation strategy in the narrow sense. Chapter 14 also introduced how project implementation strategy in the narrow sense determined the use of prequalification.

In summary, the appropriate use of both tendering and prequalification protects tender bids from incapable external contributors, on the one hand, while preventing unnecessarily narrow competition for the project work, on the other hand. Finally, the right use of tendering and prequalification as parts of project implementation strategy in the broader sense also contributes to achieving overall success in the project.

- The project implementation strategy applied in an external project has both direct and indirect impacts on bid evaluation and on the underlying bid invitation. Chapter 14 also drew attention to this phenomenon. Ranking eligible bids is a critical issue since the best bidder will become the contributor who implements the project work under the conditions of the project implementation strategy. Bid ranking should, therefore, support the project implementation strategy, while the project implementation strategy should provide the framework for bid ranking.

That is, an appropriate project implementation strategy may provide the framework for bid ranking, as well as leading to more reliable bid ranking. Reliable bid ranking also contributes to achieving success in the project.

Implications for External Contributors

The external contributor is the stakeholder who implements the project. This stakeholder, as a project-based organization should, therefore, be successful in many respects.

- Success achieved against the triangle (i.e., time, cost, and quality) is of great importance for any external contributor. When the project implementation strategy in the narrow sense is appropriate, it implies that both responsibilities and risks (associated with the project triangle) are allocated in line with both the client and the project characteristics. Tendering and prequalification should be used in accordance with the underlying project implementation strategy in the narrow sense. Thus, the external contributors should not only take and bear responsibilities and risks, but they need to be capable of managing these responsibilities and risks as well. Consequently, the external contributors are likely to achieve success against the project triangle. Being successful against the triangle increases the number of references in the contributor organization.
- A bid invitation that relies on an appropriate project implementation strategy in the broader sense makes it clear what is expected from the external contributor. In this way, an appropriate project implementation strategy contributes to making a reliable decision on the bid/no bid dilemma. The design of a tender bid, especially when bidding is preceded by prequalification, is both a time-consuming and costly undertaking. Whether or not to go forward with the preparation of prequalification plus the potential development of a tender bid means making a decision on future costs and on the engagement of qualified human resources in the contributor organization. When both tendering and prequalification are matched with the requirements of both the contract and the payment type and the implications are clearly communicated, the potential external contributors may make a reliable go/no go or bid/no bid decision.
- When an external contributor decides to go forward with prequalification or with bidding, a well-established and clearly communicated project

implementation strategy drives the potential external contributors to focus on the deciding aspects of both prequalification and the tender bid. In this way, they can prepare and develop more attractive documents for the client organization.

Taking into consideration those implications of the appropriate project implementation strategy that are considered to be advantageous for the potential external contributors, it is easy to realize that these implications are ultimately advantageous for the client organizations as well. If clients have an appropriately formulated and clearly communicated project implementation strategy, they are likely to find fewer but more capable applicants in the course of prequalification. That is, the client will receive fewer but more reliable tender bids, but the competition for the project work will not be narrowed too significantly.

An inappropriate project implementation strategy, however, could lead to a negative client-contributor relationship in the course of implementing the project. Misuse of the tools used in the course of implementing the project implementation strategy could mean that one of the primary stakeholders tries to manage the misallocated responsibilities and risks not only for their own benefit but to the disadvantage of the other stakeholders as well.

References

Alam, Mehmood, Andrew Gale, Mike Brown, and Callum Kidd. 2008. "The Development and Delivery of an Industry Led Project Management Professional Development Programme: A Case Study in Project Management Education and Success Management." *International Journal of Project Management* 26: 223–37.

Alderman, Neil, and Chris Ivory. 2007. "Partnering in Major Contracts: Paradox and Metaphor." *International Journal of Project Management* 25: 368–93.

Anantatmula, Vital S. 2008. "The Role of Technology in the Project Manager Performance Model." *Project Management Journal* 39(1): 34–38.

Andersen, Erling S, and Svein A. Jessen. 2003. "Project Maturity in Organisations." *International Journal of Project Management* 21: 457–61.

Andersen, Erling S, Kristoffer V. Grude, and Tor Haug. 2004. *Goal Directed Project Management*. London: Kogan Page.

Archer, Norman P, and Fereidoun Ghasemzadeh. 1999. "An Integrated Framework for Project Portfolio Selection." *International Journal of Project Management* 17: 207–16.

Artto, Karlos, Jaakko Kujala, Perttu Dirtrich, and Miia Martinsuo. 2008. "What is Project Strategy?" *International Journal of Project Management* 26: 4–12.

Atkinson, Roger. 1999. "Project Management: Cost, Time and Quality, Two Best Guesses and a Phenomenon, its Time to Accept Other Success Criteria." *International Journal of Project Management* 17: 337–42.

Atkinson, Roger, Lynn Crawford, and Stephen Ward. 2006. "Fundamental Uncertainties in Projects and the Scope of Project Management." *International Journal of Project Management* 24: 687–98.

Aubry, Monique, Brian Hobbs, and Denis Thuillier. 2007. "A New Framework for Understanding Organizational Project Management Through the PMO." *International Journal of Project Management* 25: 328–36.

Baccarini, David. 1999. "The Logical Framework Method for Defining Project Success." *Project Management Journal* 30(4): 25–32.

Belassi, Walid, and Oya I. Tukel. 1996. "A New Framework for Determining Critical Success/Failure Factors." *International Journal of Project Management* 14: 141-51.

Bennington, Peter, and David Baccarini. 2004. "Project Benefits Management in IT Projects—An Australian Perspective." *Project Management Journal* 35(2): 20–30.

Besner, Claude, and Brian Hobbs. 2008. "Project Management Practice, Generic or Contextual: A Reality Check." *Project Management Journal* 39(1): 16–33.

Blomquist, Tomas, and Ralf Müller. 2006. "Practices, Roles, and Responsibilities of Middle Managers in Program and Portfolio Management." *Project Management Journal* 37(1): 52–66.

Bonnal, Pierre, Didier Gourc, and Germain Lacoste. 2002. "The Life Cycle of Technical Projects." *Project Management Journal* 33(1): 12–19.

Bonnal, Pierre, Jurgen De Jonghe, and John Ferguson. 2006. "A Deliverable-Oriented EVM System Suited to a Large-Scale Project." *Project Management Journal* 37(1): 67–80.

Bower, Denise. 2003a. "The Role of Procurement in the Construction Industry." In *Management of Procurement*, edited by Denise Bower, 1–14. London: Thomas Telford.

Bower, Denise. 2003b. "Contract Strategy." In *Management of Procurement*, edited by Denise Bower 58–73. London: Thomas Telford.

Bower, Denise. 2003c. "Contractor Selection, Contract Award and Contract Law in the UK." In *Management of Procurement*, edited by Denise Bower 15–33. London: Thomas Telford.

Bower, Denise, and Nigel J. Smith. 1995. "Tender Procedures and Contract Policy." In *Engineering Project Management*, edited by Nigel J. Smith 210–28. London: Blackwell Science.

Bredillet, Christophe N. 2008. "Exploring Research in Project Management: Nine Schools of Project Management Research (Part 4)." From the Editor. *Project Management Journal* 39(1): 2–6.

Burgess, T.F., K. Byrne, and C. Kidd. 2003. "Making Project Status Visible in Complex Aerospace Projects." *International Journal of Project Management* 21: 251–59.

Cano, Juan L., and Iván Lidón. 2011. "Guided Reflection on Project Definition." *International Journal of Project Management* 29: 525–36.

CIRIA SP 15. 1981. *A Client's Guide to Design-and-Build*. London: CIRIA.

Cleden, David. 2009. *Managing Project Uncertainty*. Farnham: Gower.

Cleland, David I. 1990. *Project Management. Strategic Design and Implementation*. New York: McGraw-Hill.

Cleland, David I., and William R. King. 1975 (2nd edn.). *Systems Analysis and Project Management*. New York: McGraw-Hill.

Cleland, David I. 1994 (2nd edn.). *Project Management. Strategic Design and Implementation*. New York: McGraw-Hill.

Clifton Jr., David S., and David E. Fyffe. 1977. *Project Feasibility Analysis. A Guide to Profitable New Ventures*. New York: John Wiley and Sons.

Cooke-Davies, T. 2002. "The "Real" Success Factors on Projects." *International Journal of Project Management* 20: 185–90.

De Wit, Anton. 1988. "Measurement of Project Success." *International Journal of Project Management* 6: 164–70.

El-Sawalhi, Nabil, David Eaton, and Rifat Rustom. 2007. "Contractor Pre-qualification Model: State-of-the-Art." *International Journal of Project Management* 25: 465–74.

Fleming, Quentin W. 2003. *Project Procurement Management*. Tustin, California: FMC Press.

Fortune, Joyce, and Diana White. 2006. "Framing of Project Critical Success Factors by a System Model." *International Journal of Project Management* 24: 53–65.

Freeman, Mark, and Peter Beale. 1992. "Measuring Project Success." *Project Management Journal* 23(1): 8–17.

Gardiner, Paul D., and Kenneth Stewart. 2000. "Revisiting the Golden Triangle of Cost, Time and Quality: The Role of NPV in Project Control, Success and Failure." *International Journal of Project Management* 18: 251–56.

Gareis, Roland. 2004. *Happy Projects!* Vienna: Manz.

Gido, Jack,, and James P. Clements. 1999. *Successful Project Management*. Cincinnati, Ohio: International Thomson.

Görög, Mihály. 1993. *Bevezetés a projektmenedzsmentbe*. Budapest: Aula.

Görög, Mihály. 1996. *Általános projektmenedzsment*. Budapest: Aula.

Görög, Mihály. 2000. "Providing a Link Between Strategic Objectives and Projects." *Journal of European Business Education* 10(1): 59–69.

Görög, Mihály. 2001. "The Project Clients' Role in Achieving Project Success." *SENET Project Management Review* 2(1): 5–9.

Görög, Mihály. 2003. *A projektvezetés mestersége*. Budapest: Aula.

Görög, Mihály. 2007 (2nd edn.). *A projektvezetés mestersége*. Budapest: Aula.

Görög, Mihály. 2011. "Translating Single Project Management Knowledge to Project Programs." *Project Management Journal*, 42(2): 17–31.

Görög, Mihály, and Nigel J. Smith. 1999. *Project Management for Managers*. Sylva, Pennsylvania: PMI.

Grundy, Tony. 1998. "Strategy Implementation and Project Management." *International Journal of Project Management* 16: 43–50.

Grundy, Tony, and Laura Brown. 2002. *Strategic Project Management*. London: Thomson Learning.

Harris, Elaine. 2009. *Strategic Project Risk Appraisal and Management*. Farnham: Gower.

Hayes, Ross W., John G. Perry, Peter A. Thompson, and Gillian Willmer. 1987. *Risk Management in Engineering Construction*. London: Thomas Telford.

Jaafari, A. 2007. "Project and Program Diagnostics: A Systemic Approach." *International Journal of Project Management* 25: 781–90.

Johnson, Gerry, and Kevan Scholes. 1993 (3rd edn.). *Exploring Corporate Strategy*. Hemel Hempstead: Prentice Hall International.

Jugdev, Kam, and Ralf Müller. 2005. "A Retrospective Look at Our Evolving Understanding of Project Success." *Project Management Journal* 36(4): 19–31.

Kadefors, Anna, Emma Björlingson, and Andreas Karlsson. 2007. "Procuring Service Innovations: Contractor Selection for Partnering Projects." *International Journal of Project Management* 25: 375–85.

Kaplan, Robert S., and David P. Norton. 2004. *Strategy Maps*. Harvard Business School Publishing Corporation: Boston.

Kwak, Young H, and Frank T. Anbari. 2008. *Impact on Project Management of Allied Disciplines: Trends and Future of Project Management Practices and Research*. Newtown Square, Pennsylvania: PMI.

Lawson, Gillian. 1999. "Project Strategy and Organization." In *Project Management for the Process* Industries, edited by Gillian Lawson, Stephen Wearne, and Peter Iles-Smith, 25–47. Rugby: Institution of Chemical Engineers.

Leybourne, Stephen A. 2007. "The Changing Bias of Project Management Research: A Consideration of the Literatures and an Application of Extant Theory." *Project Management Journal* 38(1): 61–73.

Lock, Dennis. 1968. *Project Management*. Aldershot: Gower.

Lock, Dennis. 1992 (5th edn.). *Project Management*. Aldershot: Gower.

Lopes, M.D.S. and R. Flawell. 1998. "Project Appraisal—A Framework to Assess Non-financial Aspects of Projects During the Project Life Cycle." *International Journal of Project Management* 16: 223–33.

Lycett, Mark, Andreas Rassau, and John Danson. 2004. "Programme Management: A Critical Review." *International Journal of Project Management* 22: 289–99.

Marsh, Peter. 1981 (2nd edn.). *Contracting for Engineering and Constuction Projects*. Aldershot: Gower.

Marsh, Peter. 2009. "Contracts and Payment Structures." In *Contracting for Project Management* (3rd edn.), edited by Rodney J. Turner, 19–31. Farnham: Gower.

Martinsuo, Mia, and Päivi Lehtonen. 2007a. "Role of Single-project Management in Achieving Portfolio Management Efficiency." *International Journal of Project Management* 25: 56–65.

Martinsuo, Mia, and Päivi Lehtonen. 2007b. "Program and Its Initiation in Practice: Development Program Initiation in a Public Consortium." *International Journal of Project Management* 25: 337–45.

Maylor, Harvey, Tim Brady, Terry Cooke-Davies, and Damian Hodgson. 2006. "From Projectification to Programmification." *International Journal of Project Management* 24: 663–74.

McElroy, William. 1996. "Implementing Strategic Change Through Projects." *International Journal of Project Management* 14: 325–29.

Merna, Tonny, and Nigel J. Smith. 1994. *Projects Procured by Privately Financed Concession Contracts*. Manchester: UMIST.

Miller, James G. 1971. "The Nature of Living Systems." *Behavioral Science* 16: 277–301.

Milosevic, Dragan, Ross J. Martinelli, and James M. Waddell. 2007. *Program Management for Improved Business Results*. Hoboken: John Wiley & Sons.

Moore, Simon. 2009. *Strategic Project Portfolio Management: Enabling a Productive Organization*. Hoboken: John Wiley & Sons.

Morris, Peter W.G., and Ashley Jamieson. 2004. *Translating Corporate Strategy into Project Strategy*. Newtown Square, Pennsylvania: PMI.

Morris, Peter W.G., and Ashley Jamieson. 2005. "Moving from Corporate Strategy to Project Strategy." *Project Management Journal* 36(4): 5–18.

Morris, Peter W.G., and Jeffrey K. Pinto. 2007. *The Wiley Guide to Project, Program, and Portfolio Management*. Hoboken: John Wiley & Sons.

Müller, Ralf, Miia Martinsuo, and Tomas Blomquist. 2008. "Project Portfolio Control and Portfolio Management Performance in Different Context." *Project Management Journal* 39(3): 28–42.

Neal, R.A. 1995. "Project Definition: The Soft-system Approach." *International Journal of Project Management* 13: 5–9.

Olsson, Nils O.E. 2006. "Management of Flexibility in Projects." *International Journal of Project Management* 24: 66–74.

Pellegrinelli, Sergio, David Partington, Chris Hemingway, Zaher Mohdzain, and Mahmood Shah. 2007. "The Importance of Context in Programme Management: An Empirical Review of Programme Practice." *International Journal of Project Management* 25: 41–55.

Perry, John G. 1985. *Development of Contract Strategies for Construction Projects*. UMIST: PhD Thesis.

Pinto, Jeffrey K., and John E. Prescott. 1990. "Planning and Tactical Factors in Project Implementation Success." *The Journal of Management Studies* 27(3): 305–28.

Pollack, Julien. 2007. "The Changing Paradigms of Project Management." *International Journal of Project Management* 25: 266–274.

Project Management Institute. 2008 (4th edn.). *A Guide to the Project Management Body of Knowledge* (PMBOK® Guide). Newtown Square, Pennsylvania: PMI.

Rad, Parviz F., and Ginger Levin. 2006. *Project Portfolio Management: Tools and Techniques*. New York: IIL Publishing.

Schwalbe, Kathy. 2004 (3rd edn.). *Information Technology Project Management*. Boston: Thomson.

Sen, Amartya. 2009. *The Idea of Justice*. Cambridge, Massachusetts: The Belknap Press of Harvard University Press.

Shenhar, Aaron J., Dragan Milosevic, Dov Dvir, and Hans Thamhain. 2007. *Linking Project Management to Business Strategy*. Newtown Squer, Pennsylvania: PMI.

Smith, Nigel J. 1995. "Contract Strategy." In *Engineering Project Management*, edited by Nigel J. Smith, 188–209. Oxford: Blackwell Science.

Söderholm, Anders. 2008. "Project Management of Unexpected Events." *International Journal of Project Management* 26: 80–86.

Standish Group. 2009. *CHAOS summary.* Boston: Standish Group.

Steffens, Wolfgang, Miia Martinsuo, and Karlos Artto. 2007. "Change Decisions in Product Development Projects." *International Journal of Project Management* 25: 702–13.

Stewart, Rodney A. 2008. "A Framework for the Lifecycle Management of Information Technology Projects: Project IT." *International Journal of Project Management* 26: 203–12.

Tavistock Institute. 1966. *Interdependence and Uncertainty.* London: Tavistock.

Thiry, Michel. 2002. "Combining Value and Project Management into an Effective Programme Management Model." *International Journal of Project Management* 20: 221–27.

Thiry, Michel. 2004a. "How Can the Benefits of PM Training Programs Be Improved?" *International Journal of Project Management* 22: 13–18.

Thiry, Michel. 2004b. "For DAD: A Programme Management Life-cycle Process." *International Journal of Project Management* 22: 245–52.

Thiry, Michel. 2007 (4th edn.). "Managing Portfolios of Projects." In *Gower Handbook of Project Management*, edited by Rodney J. Turner, 47–70. Aldershot: Gower.

Thiry, Michel, and Manon Deguire. 2007. "Recent Developments in Project-based Organizations." *International Journal of Project Management* 25: 649–58.

Thompson, Peter A. 1981. *Organization and Economics of Construction.* Maidenhead: McGraw-Hill.

Thompson, Peter A. 1989. "Financial Control of Public Works." In *Control of Engineering Projects (2nd edn.)*, edited by Stephen Wearne, 76–98. London: Thomas Telford.

Turner, Rodney J. 1999 (2nd edn.). *The Handbook of Project-based Management: Improving the Process for Achieving Strategic Objectives.* London: McGraw-Hill.

Turner, Rodney J. 2004. "Five Necessary Conditions for Project Success." Editorial. *International Journal of Project Management* 22: 349–50.

Turner, Rodney J. 2006. "Towards a Theory of Project Management: The Nature of the Project." Editorial. *International Journal of Project Management* 24: 1–3.

Turner, Rodney J. 2009. "Farsighted Project Contract Management." In *Contracting for Project Management (3rd edn.)*, edited by Rodney J. Turner, 33–57. Farnham: Gower.

Turner, Rodney J., and Ralf Müller. 2003. "On the Nature of the Project as a Temporary Organization." *International Journal of Project Management* 21: 1–8.

van den Honert, Alex. 1994. The Strategic Connection With Project Process. *INTERNET '94 12th World Congress Proceedings*: vol. 1. 179–88.

Van Der Merve, A.P. 2002. "Project Management and Business Development: Integrating Strategy, Structure, Process and Projects." *International Journal of Project Management* 20: 401–11.

Ward, Garth. 2008. *The Project Manager's Guide to Purchasing.* Aldershot: Gower.

Wateridge, John. 1997. "How Can IS/IT Projects Be Measured for Success?" *International Journal of Project Management* 16: 59–63.

Wateridge, John. 1999. "The Role of Configuration Management in the Development and Management of Information Systems/Technology (IS/IT) Projects." *International Journal of Project Management* 17: 237–41.

Watt, D.J., B. Kayis, and K. Willey. 2009. Identifying Key Factors in the Evaluation of Tenders for Projects and Services. *International Journal of Project Management*, 27, pp. 250–260.

Watt, D.J., Kayis, B. and Willey, K. 2010. The Relative Importance of Tender Evaluation and Contractor Selection Criteria. *International Journal of Project Management*, 28, pp. 51–60.

Wearne, Stephen H. 1976. *Mechanical Engineering Contract Procedures.* London: The Institution of Mechanical Engineers.

Wearne, Stephen H. 1999. "Contracts for Goods and Services." In *Project Management for the Process Industries*, edited by Gillian Lawson, Stephen Wearne, and Peter Iles-Smith, 261–83. Rugby: Institution of Chemical Engineers.

Wheelwright, Steven C., and Kim B. Clark. 1992. "Creating Project Plans to Focus Product Development." *Harvard Business Review* (March-April) 16.

Winter, Mark, Charles Smith, Terry Cooke-Davies, and Svetlana Cicmil. 2006. "The Importance of 'Process' in Rethinking Project Management: The Story of a UK Government-funded Research Network." *International Journal of Project Management* 24: 650–62.

World Bank. 2005. *Little Data Book.* Washington DC: The World Bank Development Data Group.

Yu, Angus G., Peter D. Flett, and John A. Bowers. 2005. "Developing a Value Centered Proposal for Assessing Project Success." *International Journal of Project Management* 23: 428–36.

Index